Osbert Salvin, P. L. Scalter

A Revision of the Neotropical Anatidae

Osbert Salvin, P. L. Scalter

A Revision of the Neotropical Anatidae

ISBN/EAN: 9783741135620

Manufactured in Europe, USA, Canada, Australia, Japa

Cover: Foto ©Thomas Meinert / pixelio.de

Manufactured and distributed by brebook publishing software
(www.brebook.com)

Osbert Salvin, P. L. Scalter

A Revision of the Neotropical Anatidae

This Bolivian race of *Asturina* seems to be separable from the form already recognized, by its combination of the characters of several of its allies.   The tail is like that of the Central-American *A. ruficauda*, from which, however, it differs in the dark head and rufous chest. The underparts resemble those of *A. nattereri* ; but the head is darker, and the tail is differently coloured.   *A. pucherani* differs from the present bird in the lighter, almost creamy, colour of the underparts and primaries.

A recent examination in the Paris Museum of the specimens referred to as *Astur magnirostris* by D'Orbigny (Syn. Av. p. 5; and Voy. p. 91) proves them to belong to *Asturina pucherani* as defined in our synopsis of the genus *Asturina* (P. Z. S. 1869, p. 133, and Exot. Orn. p. 177, t. 89); though from D'Orbigny's remarks upon them we were previously in some doubt on this point.

5. A Revision of the Neotropical Anatidæ.   By P. L. Sclater, M.A., Ph.D., F.R.S., and Osbert Salvin, M.A., F.R.S.

[Received April 4, 1876.]

(Plate XXXIV.)

I. Introduction.

The greater part of this paper was written before the issue of the 'Nomenclator Avium Neotropicalium' in 1873; and the systematic arrangement of the genera and species of Anatidæ adopted in the 'Nomenclator' was taken from the MS., which was laid aside unfinished in consequence of the pressure of other matters.   It has now been thought desirable to complete it for publication, in order to show the ground upon which certain species were included in the list, and in order to give a more complete account of the geographical distribution of the South-American Anatidæ than has yet appeared. Certain necessary changes in the nomenclature have been introduced.

As only a small portion of this widely distributed family is treated of here, no attempt has been made to propound any new classifications, but that in ordinary use has been followed.

It has not been thought necessary to give descriptions of the species contained in Baird's 'Birds of North America.'

II. Preliminary Remarks on the Neotropical Anatidæ.

The Anatidæ of the southern portion of the South-American continent differ greatly, both as to genera and species, from the members of the same group of birds found on the northern confines of the Neotropical fauna.   The former are most of them peculiar to

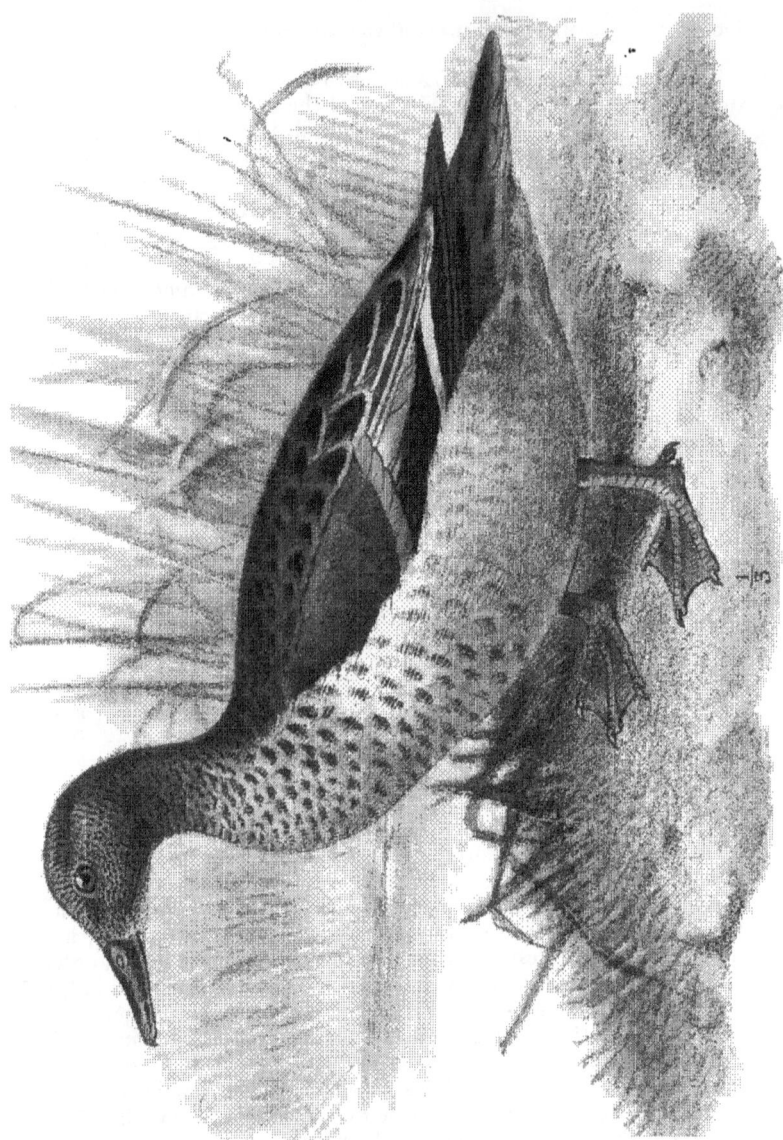

the districts in which they are found, whilst the latter, with few ex-
ceptions, consist of winter emigrants from the northern continent.
In the intermediate country, comprising by far the larger portion of
South America, few members of this family are met with. In speaking
of the Anatidæ of the Neotropical Region, therefore, our subject very
naturally divides itself into two portions, each of which requires
somewhat different treatment, owing to the amount of attention they
have received from naturalists. We propose, then, to give a more
complete account of those species which belong strictly to the
southern continent, including the Antilles and Central America
with Mexico. The species which belong to the northern continent
and which only come during winter within the limits of the South-
American avifauna, on the other hand, we shall handle more briefly,
confining our notes and references to such as bear upon their occurrence in their winter quarters.

The geographical distribution of the South-American Anatidæ
requires special consideration, inasmuch as the members of this
family found in the Neotropical region, except in a few cases, do
not conform in their range to the limits assigned to that region, but
to a great extent rally round the more temperate portions of the
continent. The characteristic species are in no case met with near
the northern boundaries of the Neotropical region.

The equatorial genera *Dendrocygna* and *Cairina*, however, reach
Southern Mexico; and the former is represented throughout the
Antilles. They alone are distributed according to the prevailing
law affecting Neotropical birds. Intertropical countries in general
are not rich in Anatidæ; and America is no exception to the rule.
The Tree-ducks (*Dendrocygna*) form the chief exception. They
alone abound in Tropical America, the high Andes (tropical only in
position) being, of course, left out of consideration. The cause of this
scarcity is not very apparent at first sight. The enormous rivers of
tropical America and its numberless lagoons might be expected to
be capable of supporting Ducks in any quantity. But such is not
the case. The intertropical species are almost all of them arboreal
in their habits; and it may possibly be that this is so because they
thus escape being preyed upon by the large Crocodilians which
abound in these waters.

The bulk of the peculiar South-American species are not found to
the northward of the lower portion of the basin of the La Plata.
Here, however, and onwards to Tierra del Fuego they abound, not
only in species but in individuals, and their numbers would seem to
rival those of the northern hemisphere. But the component species,
and, in many instances, the genera, are quite different. Swans are
there, but the species bear no resemblance to those of the north.
The Geese are all different. *Anas* is there, but differing widely from
the northern prototype. The same may be said of *Dafila*, where the
sexes are similarly dressed, instead of being widely different. *Mareca*
is also there; but here, again, the sexes are nearly alike, instead of
the reverse. The Teals, too, of the south are very different from
those of the north. The host of northern diving and oceanic species

ᵃre doubtfully represented by the two aberrant genera *Metopiana* and *Tachyeres*; and the Andean *Merganetta* stands quite alone.

The Shovellers (*Spatula*) of north and south are strictly congeneric; so also are the members of the genera *Erismatura* and *Mergus*.

Returning to the strictly tropical members of this family, and tracing their alliances and range, we find some remarkable facts in geographical distribution, which, so far as we are aware, find no parallel amongst birds. The genus *Chenalopex* contains but two species—one belonging to the valley of the Amazons and the adjoining districts, the other to Africa. *Sarcidiornis* is found in Paraguay, Africa, Madagascar, the peninsula of India, Ceylon, and Burmah. *Dendrocygna viduata* is common to both the American and African continents; and *D. fulva* is found alike in America, India, and Madagascar. The causes of this singular distribution of so many members of one family are at present inexplicable.

The greater part of our characters in the following synopsis are taken from specimens in the collection of Salvin and Godman, which contains most of the known South-American species. In selecting specimens for description we have sought out such as came from the same or the nearest locality to that where the original types were procured.

III. SYNOPSIS OF THE SPECIES OF NEOTROPICAL ANATIDÆ.

The Anatidæ may be divided into the following seven subfamilies:—

  I. *Anserinæ* or Geese.
  II. *Cygninæ* or Swans.
  III. *Anatinæ* or River-ducks.
  IV. *Fuligulinæ* or Sea-ducks.
  V. *Erismaturinæ* or Lake-ducks.
  VI. *Merganettinæ*, or Torrent-ducks.
  VII. *Merginæ* or Mergansers.

Subfamily I. ANSERINÆ.

Genus 1. ANSER.   Type.

Anser, Cuv. Règn. An. i. p. 530 (1817) ...... *A. cinereus*.
Chen, Boié, Isis, 1822, p. 563 .... *A. hyperboreus*.

Anser is strictly an arctopolitan form, of which winter visitants belonging to three species occur in the Antilles.

1. ANSER HYPERBOREUS.

Anser hyperboreus, Pallas, Spic. Zool. vi. p. 31 (1769); Zoogr. vol. ii. p. 227, t. 65; Baird, B. of N. Am. p. 760 (1858); Cab. J. für Orn. 1857, p. 225 (Cuba); March, Pr. Ac. Phil. 1864, p. 70 (Jamaica).

  Chen hyperboreus, Gundl. Repert. F.-N. i. p. 387, et J. für Orn. 1875, p. 371 (Cuba).

  Hab. Cuba (*Gundlach*); Jamaica (*March*).

In Cuba *A. hyperboreus* seems to be a regular annual visitant, and is common, remaining in the island from October until the end of March. It has only been observed in Jamaica when the winter in the north has been severe.

2. ANSER CÆRULESCENS.

Anas cærulescens, Linn. S. N. i. p. 198 (1766).
Anser cærulescens, Elliot, B. of N. Am. t. 43; Bryant, Pr. Bost. Soc. N. II. xi. (1866) p. 70 (Inagua).
Chen cærulescens, Gundl. Repert. F.-N. i. p. 387, et J. für Orn. 1875, p. 374 (Cuba).

Hab. Inagua, Bahama Island (*Bryant*); Cuba (*Gundlach*).

Dr. Bryant reports that, some years before his visit to Inagua in 1859, a flock of this Goose visited the island, when every individual was killed by the inhabitants. Dr. Gundlach, who maintains the distinctness between this bird and *A. hyperboreus*, says that it is of rare occurrence in Cuba, but that it arrives along with the migratory flocks of the allied species.

3. ANSER GAMBELI.

Anser gambelii, Hartl. Rev. Zool. 1852, p. 7; Baird, B. of N. Am. p. 761 (1858); Cab. J. für Orn. 1857, p. 226 (Cuba); Gundl. Repert. F.-N. i. p. 387, et J. für Orn. 1875, p. 375 (Cuba); Lawr. Mem. Bost. Soc. N. H. ii. p. 313 (Mazatlan).

Hab. Cuba (*Gundlach*); Mazatlan (*Grayson*).

Not common, but not so rare in Cuba as *A. cærulescens*, where, however, it is stated to be a regular winter visitant, remaining in the island from October till the end of March. Col. Grayson obtained it near Mazatlan, N.W. Mexico.

Genus 2. BERNICLA.

		Type.
*Bernicla**, Boié, Isis, 1822, p. 563	*B. torquata*	
	(= *B. canadensis*).	
Chloëphaga, Eyton, Mon. Anatidæ, p. 13 (1838)	*B. magellanica.*	
Tænidiestes, Reich. Nat. Syst. d. Vög. p. ix (1852)	*B. antarctica.*	
Chlætrophus, Bannister, Pr. Ac. Sc. Phil. 1870, p. 131	*B. poliocephala.*	
Oressochen, Bannister, Pr. Ac. Sc. Phil. 1870, p. 131	*B. melanoptera.*	

Bernicla is a widely extended form, with four or five representatives in North America, of which one reaches the Neotropical region as an

---

* Some attempts have recently been made to revive *Branta* of Scopoli (Ann. I. II. N. p. 67) for this genus. But *Branta* of Scopoli is an artificial group composed of species which have no sort of natural affinity, and is therefore to be cancelled. Besides *Branta* is generally used for *Fuligula rufina*, and it would create great confusion to substitute it for the universally accepted term *Bernicla*.

occasional winter visitant, and with six peculiar species in Antarctic America.

1. BERNICLA CANADENSIS.

Anas canadensis, Linn. S. N. i. p. 198 (1766).
Bernicla canadensis, Baird, B. of N. Am. p. 764 (1858); March, Proc. Ac. Phil. 1864, p. 70 (Jamaica); A. & E. Newton, Ibis, 1859, p. 368 (St. Croix?).
Anser parvipes, Cass. Pr. Ac. Phil. vi. p. 188 (1852), (Vera Cruz).
Bernicla canadensis, var. *occidentalis*, Lawr. Mem. Bost. Soc. N. H. ii. p. 271 (Durango).
Hab. Jamaica (*March*); Durango, Mexico (*Grayson*).

An occasional visitant in Jamaica in winter, its occurrence depending upon the rigour of that season in the north. Messrs. A. & E. Newton think that a flock of wild Geese seen in the Island of St. Croix in 1857 probably belonged to this species. *Anser parvipes*, from Vera Cruz, is only known to us from Cassin's description, but may probably belong to *B. canadensis*. Durango is the only other recorded Mexican locality for it. Col. Grayson here met with it.

2. BERNICLA MELANOPTERA.

Anser melanopterus, Eyton, Mon. Anat. p. 93 (1838) (Lake Titicaca); Darwin, Voy. Beagle, iii. p. 134, t. 50 (1841); Schl. Mus. des P.-B., Anseres, p. 100; Tschudi, F. P. p. 308 (1846) (Puna reg. of Peru).
Bernicla melanoptera, Gay, Faun. Chil. p. 443 (1848) (Chili); Reich. Natat. lviii. f. 953; Bibra, Denkschr. Akad. Wien, v. p. 131; cf. J. für Orn. 1855, p. 57 (Chili); Cassin, Gilliss's Exp. ii. p. 101 (1856) (Chili); Phil. & Landb. Wiegm. Arch. 1863, p. 185, et Cat. Av Chil. p. 40 (Chili); Scl. Ibis, 1864, p. 121; P. Z. S. 1867, pp. 320, 334, 339 (Chili); Scl. & Salv. P. Z. S. 1869, p. 156 (Pitumarca).
Chloëphaga melanoptera, Burm. La Plata-Reise, ii. p. 513, et P. Z. S. 1872, p. 365.
Oressochen melanopterus, Bannister, Proc. Ac. Phil. 1870, p. 131.
Anser montanus, Tsch. Wiegm. Arch. ix. pt. i. p. 390.
Anser anticola, Tsch. Wiegm. Arch. x. pt. i. p. 315 (1844).

Alba; remigibus nigris; scapularibus et cauda viridescenti-nigris; tectricibus alarum majoribus extus purpureis, speculum formantibus; minoribus albis; scapularibus anterioribus fusco notatis, posterioribus fuscis in viridescenti-nigrum trahentibus: long. tota circ. 30, alæ 17·5, caudæ 6·5, rostri a rictu 1·7, tarsi 3·7, dig. med. cum ungue 3·3 (Descr. exempl. ex Peruviâ in Mus. S. & G.): *rostro (ave vivâ) carneo, ungue nigricante, pedibus rubris, irideo bscura. Fem. mari similis, sed minor.*
Hab. Lake Titicaca (*King, Pentland*); Puna region of Peru (*Tschudi*); Tinta, S. Peru (*Whitely*); cordillera and plains of Chili (*Ph. et Landb.*); Quintero, Chili (*Gay*); Portillo Pass, Chili (*Gilliss*).

This fine goose is found in the high Andes of Peru and Bolivia, and has been observed both on Lake Titicaca and at Tinta and Pitumarca, at an elevation of from 11,000 to 14,000 feet above the sea-level, in what Tschudi has termed the "Puna region." It is also found throughout the central provinces of Chili, descending to the plains in winter, but in summer retiring to the high Cordillera, to the verge of the line of perpetual snow. It has been observed at Quintero, in the province of Santiago, and in such numbers, on a small body of water near the celebrated Portillo Pass, that the spot is called Valle de los Pinquenes, Pinquen being the native name of this species. The limit of its southern range probably hardly passes the 35th degree of south latitude.

There were three specimens of this fine species lately living in the menagerie of this Society (List Vert. Zool. Soc. 1872, p. 244); but none of them seemed to enjoy such good health in captivity as the other South-American Geese. The male is considerably larger than the female.

3. BERNICLA MAGELLANICA.

Oie des Terres magellaniques, Buff. Pl. Enl. 1006, unde

Anas magellanica, Gm. S. N. i. p. 505 (1788) (Straits of Magellan).

Anser pictus et *magellanicus*, Vieill. Enc. Méth. p. 117 (1823).

Chloëphaga magellanica, Eyton, Mon. Anat. p. 82 (1838); Darwin, Voy. Beagle, iii. p. 134 (1841) (Tierra del Fuego and Falkland Islands): Scl. P. Z. S. 1857, p. 128; 1858, p. 289; 1860, p. 387 (Falkland Islands); Gould, P. Z. S. 1859, p. 96; Abbott, Ibis, 1861, p. 157 (Falkland Islands); Scl. & Salv. Ibis, 1868, p. 189 (Straits of Magellan); 1870, p. 500 (Elizabeth Isle); Ph. & Landb. Cat. Av. Chil. p. 40.

Bernicla magellanica, Gay, Fauna Chil. p. 443 (1848) (Chiloe).

Painted Duck, Cook, It. i. p. 96, unde

Anas picta, Gm. S. N. i. p. 504 (1788) (Staaten Island).

Anas leucoptera, Gm. S. N. i. p. 505 (1788); ex Buff. xvii. p. 101, et Brown's Ill. t. 40 (Falkland Islands).

Anser leucopterus, Vieill. Enc. Méth. p. 113 (1823).

Bernicla leucoptera, Less. Traité d'Orn. p. 627 (1831).

*Alba, hypochondriis et dorso superiore cum parte basali colli postici nigro transvittatis; primariis, tectricibus alarum majoribus, tertiariis et scapularibus elongatis cinerascentibus; dorso postico et rectricibus cinerascenti-nigris; rostro nigro, iride fere nigra, pedibus obscure plumbeis: long. tota circ. 26, alæ 16·3, caudæ 5·5, rostri a rictu 1·6, tarsi 3·8, dig. med. cum ungue 3·3.
Fem. capite et collo cinnamomeis; gastræo antice cinnamomeo, postice albo, omnino nigro transvittato; subcaudalibus lateralibus nigris, mediis fusco irroratis; dorso antico cervino et albo transvittato, postico et rectricibus brunnescenti-nigris: primariis fusco-nigris, secundariis albis, tertiariis et scapularibus elongatis grisescentibus; tectricibus alarum majoribus æneis, vitta subapicali nigra, albo terminatis; rostro nigro,*

iride fere nigra, pedibus flavis: long. tota circ. 26, alæ 16, *caudæ* 5·5, *rostri a rictu* 1·6, *tarsi* 3·3, *dig. med. cum ung.* 3 (Descr. exempl. ex Ins. Falklandici in Mus. S. & G.).

Hab. Straits of Magellan (*King, Darwin, Cunningham*) : Staaten Island (*Cook*) : Falkland Islands (*Darwin, Abbott*).

According to Darwin, this Goose is found in Tierra del Fuego and the Falkland Islands, being common in the latter. They live in pairs or small flocks in the interior of the island, and seldom approach either the sea or the freshwater lakes. They build on the outlying islets, probably through fear of the foxes ; and the same cause may also account for their being tame by day but the reverse on the approach of dusk. They live entirely on vegetable matter, and are called by the seamen " Upland Geese."

Capt. Abbott, who, like other travellers, found this species common in East Falkland, says that it breeds all over the country, as well as on the adjoining islets—and on this point differs from Mr. Darwin ; but he adds that the disappearance of foxes from East Falkland may have led to a change of habits as regards the situation chosen by this species for its nest. He gives a good account of its nesting-habits.

This species appears to do well in captivity, and many broods have been reared in the Gardens of this Society since its introduction in 1857 (Rev. List of Vert. Zool. Soc. 1872, p. 245).

The Chilian form of this Goose has been described by Philippi and Landbeck as *Bernicla dispar*—the main and, in fact, the only distinction consisting in the male being distinctly barred with black on the under surface. Our immature male specimen from the Falklands is marked to a slight extent in a similar manner ; and we are disposed to consider the character one of hardly sufficient value to separate the two forms specifically. The following references belong to the Chilian form :—

4. BERNICLA DISPAR.

Bernicla magellanica, Cassin, Gilliss's Exp. ii. p. 201, t. xxiv. (1856); Gay, Fauna Chil. p. 413 (1848) (Chiloe).

Bernicla dispar, Ph. & Landb. Wiegm. Arch. 1863, p. 190, et Cat. Av. Chil. p. 40; Burm. P. Z. S. 1872, p. 366 ; Sclater, Ibis, 1864, p. 122.

Chloëphaga dispar, Scl. P. Z. S. 1867, pp. 320, 334.

Hab. Central Chili (*Ph. et Landb.*) ; Argentine Republic, Sierra Tinta and Rio Negro (*Burm.*).

Philippi and Landbeck state that this Goose is of frequent occurrence in winter in the central provinces of Chili, and that one of the collectors for the Museum of Santiago brought a specimen from the Straits of Magellan.

Burmeister refers the Goose frequenting the Sierra Tinta, near Tandil, to the southward of Buenos Ayres, to this species or race ; he also adds that he has recently received both sexes from El Carmen, on the Rio Negro.

In October 1871 the Society purchased of Mr. Weisshaupt, along

with other Chilian animals, a pair of this form of the Magellanic
Goose. The female unfortunately died ; but the male was lent to a
correspondent, who returned to the Gardens in its place, in November
1875, a pair of young birds, bred between it and a female *B. magellanica vera*, of which we exhibit a drawing. The male, it will be
observed, is not quite so strongly barred as in the pure *B. dispar*,
but presents well-defined black edgings on the under plumage. The
females of the two forms are, so far as we can see, quite identical.

a, Male, and *b*, Female, Magellanic Geese in the Society's Gardens, bred
between *B. dispar* ♂ and *B. magellanica* ♀.

5. BERNICLA POLIOCEPHALA.

Anas inornatus ♀, King, P. Z. S. 1830-31, p. 15 (Straits of Magellan).

Bernicla inornata, Gray & Mitch. Gen. B. t. 165; Gay, Faun. Chil. i. p. 444.

Chloëphaga poliocephala, Gray, List Gall. Grall. and Anseres in B. M. p. 127 (1844), descr. nulla; Scl. P. Z. S. 1857, p. 128; 1858, p. 290; 1861, p. 46 (Falkland Islands); 1867, p. 335; Abbott, Ibis, 1861, p. 159 (Falkland Islands); Scl. & Salv. Ibis, 1868, p. 189 (Oazy Harbour); 1870, p. 499 (Port Grappler); Nomencl. p. 128.

Bernicla poliocephala, Burm. P. Z. S. 1872, p. 366 (Bahia Blanca).

Anser poliocephalus, Schl. Mus. des P.-B., Anseres, p. 101.

Chlœtrophus poliocephalus, Bann. Pr. Ac. Phil. 1870, p. 131.

Bernicla chiloensis, Ph. & Landb. Wiegm. Arch. 1863, p. 149 (Chiloe), et Cat. Av. Chil. p. 40.

Capite toto et collo cum scapularibus griseo-plumbeis, pectore et dorso superiore castaneis nigro transfasciatis; abdomine, tectricibus subalaribus, campterio et tectricibus minoribus albis; primariis nigris; secundariis albis, interioribus fusco in pogonio externo notatis; tectricibus alarum majoribus nigris, extus viridescenti-nitentibus, apicibus albis; dorso imo et cauda nigris, hypochondriis nigro et albo transfasciatis, crisso castaneo; rostro nigro, pedibus extus flavis intus fusco-nigris: long. tota 24, alæ 13·5, caudæ 5, tarsi 2·7, dig. med. cum ung. 2·5 (Descr. maris ex Patagonia (Rio Negro) in Mus. S. & G.). Fem. mari similis.

Hab. Straits of Magellan (*King, Cunningham*); Patagonia, Rio Negro (*Hudson*); Chiloe (*Philippi & Landbeck*); Falkland Islands (*Abbott, Leconte*).

This species was at first supposed to be the female of the bird described by Captain King as *Anas inornatus*, under which name an excellent figure of it was given by Gray and Mitchell in the 'Genera of Birds.' Mr. Gray was the first to detect the error and to give the present bird a MS. name; but he left it to Sclater to describe the species and make the distinctions clear. The fact of the similarity of the sexes in this and the next species has been abundantly shown by living birds which have reared broods in captivity in our Gardens. The species does not seem to be very common in the far south, as it escaped Mr. Darwin's notice; and in the Falkland Islands, the great rendezvous of these Geese, it would appear to be only a straggler.

During the three years Captain Abbott resided in the Falkland Islands he only observed three examples of this species; and these were obtained singly amongst flocks of " Upland Geese" (*B. magellanica*): he supposes that these birds were stragglers from the const of Patagonia. F. Leconte, who was sent by this Society to the Falklands to obtain living animals, brought home one skin of this Goose.

Burmeister says the range of this Goose extends over the whole of Patagonia, where it is one of the most common species.

Philippi and Landbeck state that the true patria of their *B. chiloensis* is the island of Chiloe, where it breeds. During the winter it migrates further northward. At Ancud it may be seen in a domesticated state.

Dr. Cunningham obtained this Goose at Oazy Harbour, in the Straits of Magellan, but did not meet with it in the Falkland Islands.

6. BERNICLA RUBIDICEPS.

Bernicla inornata, Gray, Zool. Voy. Erebus and Terror, t. 24.
Chloëphaga rubidiceps, Scl. P. Z. S. 1860, p. 387, t. 163 (Falkland Islands); 1861, p. 46; Abbott, Ibis, 1861, p. 158 (Falkland Islands); Scl. et Salv. Nomencl. p. 128; Sharpe, Zool. Erebus and Terror, Birds, p. 37.
Anser rubidiceps, Schl. Mus. des P.-B., Anseres, p. 102.
Chlœtrophus rubidiceps, Bann. Pr. Ac. Phil. 1870, p. 131.

Corpore subtus cum capite toto et collo cinnamomeis, pectore et hypochondriis nigro transfasciatis, crisso nigro marginato; supra grisescens colli basi crebre nigro et cinnamomeo transfasciata, interscapulii plumis fascia subterminali nigra notatis; dorso imo, uropygio et cauda nigris viridescente vix tinctis; remigibus nigris, secundariis et tectricibus alarum minoribus albis; tectricibus majoribus extus æneo-viridibus albo terminatis: long. tota circ. 23, alæ 13·5, caudæ 4·5, rostri a rictu 1·5, tarsi 2·5, dig. med. cum ungue 2·8 (Descr. maris ex insulis Falklandicis in Mus. S. & G.). *Rostro nigro, iride fere nigra, tarsis extus flavis intus nigrescentibus* (Desc. av. in vivario Zool. Soc. Lond.).

Hab. Falkland Islands (*Abbott, Leconte*).

The "Brent Goose," as this species is called in the Falkland Islands, Captain Abbott says, is not so common as the other species, except in some places in the North Camp, where he saw large numbers in pairs.

The male is larger than the female, and frequents the edge of the nearest pool of water whilst the female is sitting on her nest amongst dry bushes. The eggs are usually five (rarely six) in number, and are laid the first week in October. The young birds attain the dress of maturity the first year, except that the wing-speculum is dull black instead of glossy green.

This species also does well in captivity, many broods having been reared since 1860, when the species was first introduced into this country alive (Rev. List of Vert. Zool. Soc. 1872, p. 245).

7. BERNICLA ANTARCTICA*.

Antarctic Goose, Forst. It. pp. 495, 518, unde

* BERNICLA INORNATA.
Anas inornatus, King, P. Z. S. 1830–31, p. 15 (Straits of Magellan).
Bernicla inornata, Gay, Faun. Chil. p. 444 (1856); Gray and Sharpe, Zool. Erebus and Terror, Birds, pl. 30.
Chloëphaga inornata, Scl. et Salv. Nomencl. p. 128; Sharpe, Zool. Erebus and Terror, Birds, p. 37.
Similis præcedenti sed minor. dorso angustius transfasciato; speculo alari,

Anas antarctica, Gm. S. N. i. p. 505 (1788) (Tierra del Fuego);
Schl. Mus. des P.-B., Anseres, p. 98.
Bernicla antarctica, Steph. Shaw's Zool. xii. p. 59; Eyton, Mon.
Anat. p. 84 (1838); Darwin, Voy. Beagle, iii. p. 134 (1841)
(Tierra del Fuego, Falkland Islands); Less. Voy. Coq. t. 50; Gay,
Fauna Chil. p. 442 (1848); Reich. Natat. lvii. f. 397, 948; Bibra,
Denkschr. Akad. Wien, v. p. 131 (Chili); *cf.* J. für Orn. 1855,
p. 57; Cassin, Gilliss's Exp. ii. p. 200, t. xxiii. (1856) (coast of
Chili); 1860, p. 388; 1867, pp. 320, 334, 339; Gould, P. Z. S.
1859, p. 96; Scl. & Salv. Ibis, 1869, p. 284 (Port Otway); 1870,
p. 499 (Goods Bay); Nomencl. p. 128; Abbott, Ibis, 1861, p. 159
(Falkland Islands); Burm. La Plata-Reise, ii. p. 514, et P. Z. S.
1872, p. 366; Ph. & Landb. Wiegm. Arch. 1863, p. 199, et Cat.
Av. Chil. p. 40.
Tæniadestes antarctica, Bannister, Pr. Ac. Phil. 1870, p. 132.
Anas hybrida, Mol. Storia, p. 213 (?); Gm. S. N. i. p. 502
(1788), ex Molina.
Anas magellanicus, Sparrm. Mus. Carls. t. 37.

Mas *alba; rostro nigro, pedibus flavis: long. tota circ.* 24·0, *alæ*
15·0, *caudæ* 5·2, *rostri a rictu* 1·7, *tarsi* 3, *dig. med. cum ungue*
3·5 (Descr. exempl. vix adult. ex ins. Falklandicis in Mus.
S. & G.). Fem. *brunneo-nigra; vertice et nucha brunneis,
fronte, capitis lateribus et collo albo vermiculatis; dorso postico,
uropygio et cauda albis; primariis nigris, secundariis et tectricibus alarum minoribus cum subalaribus albis; tectricibus
majoribus viridescente extus terminatis, speculum alare formantibus: subtus pectore hypochondriis et ventre summo distincte
albo transfasciatis, ventre imo cum crisso albis: long. tota circ.*
24·0, *alæ* 14·0, *caudæ* 5·3, *rostri a rictu* 1·7, *tarsi* 2·7, *dig.
med. cum ungue* 3·2 (Descr. exempl. ex ins. Falklandicis in
Mus. S. & G.).

Hab. Tierra del Fuego (*Forster, Darwin, Cunningham*); Straits
of Magellan to Chiloe (*Darwin, Philippi & Landbeck*); Patagonia
(*Burmeister, Hudson*); Falkland Islands (*Darwin, Abbott*).

This is one of the oldest known species of South-American *Anatidæ*, being alluded to by Forster and also apparently by the Abbé
Molina, as well as in Pernety's 'Voyage.' The remarks of the first
author led to the name given to it by Gmelin, by which it has since

<hr>

dorso imo et rectricibus fusco-nigris; pedibus flavis: long. tot. circ. 24, *alæ*
14·8, *cauda* 4·5, *tarsi* 3, *dig. med. cum ungue* 2·5, *rostri a rictu* 1·2.
Hab. Straits of Magellan (*King*).
Though the type specimen of this bird in the British Museum bears a general
resemblance to a male *B. magellanica*, we are by no means sure that it may
not ultimately prove to be merely an immature specimen of *Bernicla antarctica*,
the size of the bill corresponding more closely with that of the last-named
species. From this, however, it differs in having a black tail, and in other
minor characters. The specimen is evidently immature; but not being able
to assign it positively to any other species, we leave it for the present to
stand as doubtful; at the same time we think it more than probable that it
will eventually be found to belong to one of the above-mentioned *Bernicla*.

been almost universally recognized.   The bird described by Molina,
and called *Anas hybrida*, which name was also adopted by Gmelin
as apparently applying to a species distinct from his *A. antarctica*,
probably refers to this species; and if so, Molina's name has the
priority; but so vague are his descriptions, and so inapplicable the
name he has chosen, that we must decline to disturb a title so firmly
established as *antarctica*.   Forster noticed this species in Tierra del
Fuego, where it has since been seen by every traveller who has written
on the birds of that district.   Here Darwin found it, and also in the
Falkland Islands and on the western coast of South America as far
north as Chiloe.   It lives exclusively on rocky parts of the sea-coast;
hence the name, "Rock-Goose," given to it by sailors.   In the deep
and retired channels of Tierra del Fuego, says Mr. Darwin, the snow-
white male, invariably accompanied by his darker consort, and
standing close by each other on some distant rocky point, is a common
feature in the landscape.

Captain Abbott confirms Mr. Darwin's observation as to the
abundance of this Goose in the Falklands; he adds that he found it
along the coast, and that the nest is placed a few yards from the
shore, in an exposed place, and the female may sometimes be seen
sitting on her eggs from a distance.   The male bird remains sta-
tioned close by.   The eggs are generally six or seven in number,
and, during the absence of the female, are carefully covered with
down from her breast.

Philippi and Landbeck give to this species the same range along
the west coast as Mr. Darwin, adding that it is occasionally seen at
Valdivia.   Its eastern range, according to Burmeister's latest obser-
vations, does not extend northward of the inlet of Santa Cruz, where
it winters.

Little success has at present attended the efforts to introduce this
species into England.   One individual has reached this country alive
up to the present time.   (See Rev. List of Vert. 1872, p. 245.)

Genus 3. CHENALOPEX.

Type.

Chenalopex *, Stephens, Gen. Zool. xii. pt. 2,
   p. 41 (1824) .... *C. ægyptiaca.*

CHENALOPEX JUBATA.

Anser jubatus, Spix, Av. Bras. ii. p. 84, t. 108 (1825); Burm.
Syst. Ueb. iii. p. 433.

Chenalopex jubata, Gray & Mitch. Gen. B. t. 164; Cab. in
Schomb. Guiana, iii. p. 762; J. E Gray, Knowsl. Menag. ii. t. xv.;
Taylor, Ibis, 1864, p. 96 (Orinoco); Scl. & Salv. P. Z. S. 1866, p.
200 (Ucayali); Nomencl. p. 128; Pelz. Orn. Bras. p. 319.

Sarkidiornis jubata, Gray, Hand-l. iii. p. 74.

---

* Mr. G. R. Gray (Hand-l. iii. p. 74) refers to "*Chenonetta*, Brandt, 1836," as
synonymous with *Chenalopex*.   But *Chenonetta* was proposed by Brandt (Descr.
et Ic. An. Ross. fasc. i. p. 5) for *Anas jubata*, Latham, of Australia, not for
Anser jubatus, Spix.

Anser polycomus, Cuv. in Mus. Paris; Less. Traité d'Orn. i. p. 627 (1831); Schl. Mus. des P.-B. Anseres, p. 95.
Anser pollicaris, Licht. in Mus. Berol.
Chenalopex pollicaris, Licht. Nomencl. p. 101.

Capite toto cum collo et pectore sordide albis, collo postico obscuriore; interscapulio fusco-nigro; dorso antico, scapularibus et hypochondriis castaneis; dorso imo alis et cauda purpurascenti-nigris, secundariis quinque internis macula magna alba, speculum alare formantibus, ornatis: tectricibus alarum majoribus viridescenti-nitentibus; abdomine medio et crisso albis, ventre imo utrinque nigro; rostro nigro mandibula nisi in apice flava; pedibus flavidis: long. totæ 20, alæ 11·5, caudæ 3·7, tarsi 3·7, dig. med. cum ungue 2·4 (Desc. spec. ex Amazonia Peruviana in Mus. S. & G.).

Hab. Valley of the Amazons (*Spix, Bartlett*); Guiana (*Schomburgk*); Orinoco (*Taylor*); Caiçara, Rio Guaporé et Rio Negro (*Natterer*).

The range of the species is restricted to the low-lying districts of the valley of the Amazons, and the adjoining countries of Guiana and Venezuela on the Orinoco, where, however, especially in the former region, it would appear to be abundant. Natterer obtained eight specimens during his journey, some on the head waters of the Madeira in Matogrosso, others on the Rio Negro.

Little has been recorded of the habits of this Goose. Schomburgk met with it in pairs frequenting sand banks; and Natterer states that the stomach of one he examined contained small seeds.

This species has its nearest ally in *C. ægyptiaca* of the African continent, with which it would appear to be strictly congeneric.

Subfamily II. CYGNINÆ.

Genus 1. CYGNUS. Type.

Cygnus, Meyer, Tasch. d. d. Vög. ii. p. 497 (1810)		*C. olor.*
Olor, Wagl. Isis, 1832, p. 1234		*C. musicus.*
Chenopsis, Wagl. Isis, 1832, p. 1234		*C. atratus.*
Coscoroba, Reich. Nat. Syst. d. Vög. p. x. (1852)		*C. coscoroba.*

Two species of Swan, both very distinct from any of their northern congeners, are found in Antarctic America.

1. CYGNUS NIGRICOLLIS.

Anas nigricollis, Gm. S. N. i. p. 502 (1788), ex Bougainville.
Anas melanocephala, Gm. S. N. i. p. 502 (1788), ex Molina.
Anas melanocorypha, Mol. Saggio, ed. 2, p. 199 (1810).
Anser melanocoryphus, Vieill. Enc. Méth. p. 108 (1823) ex Molina.
Cygnus nigricollis, Steph. Shaw's Zool. xii. p. 17; Eyton, Mon. p. 98 (1838); Hartl. Ind. Az. p. 27; Gay, Faun. Chil. p. 445, t. 14 (1848); Burm. Syst. Ueb. iii. p. 432; La Plata-Reise, ii. p. 512; Journ. für Orn. 1860, p. 266, et P. Z. S. 1872, p. 365;

Bibra, Denkschr. Akad. Wien, v. p. 131 ; cf. J. für Orn. 1855, p.
57 ; Scl. P. Z. S. 1859, p. 206, 1860, p. 388, 1867, pp. 334, 339 ;
Abbott, Ibis, 1860, p. 159 ; Ph. & Landb. Cat. Av. Chil. p. 50 ;
Scl. & Salv. P. Z. S. 1868, p. 145, et Ibis, 1869, p. 284 (Elizabeth
Isle), et Nomencl. p. 139.

Cisne de cabeza negra, Az. Apunt. no. 425.

*Albus; capite et collo cum striga postoculari et mento nigris ;
loris nudis : long. tota circ. 48·0 poll. angl., alæ 17·5, caudæ
5·5, rostri a rictu 3·0, tarsi 3·5, dig. med. cum ungue 4.2*
(Descr. exempl. ex inss. Falklandicis in Mus. S. & G.). *Rostro
plumbeo, ungue albo; cera tumida ruberrima ; iride fere nigra,
pedibus pallide carneis (ave viva).*

Hab. Falkland Islands (*Abbott*); Straits of Magellan (*Bougainville,
Cunningham*); La Plata (*Azara, Burmeister*); Chili (*Gay, Philippi
& Landbeck*).

This Swan is abundant in the pampas of Buenos Ayres, and in
the lower portion of the Argentine Republic, and thence southwards
to Tierra del Fuego. It is also found in the Falkland Islands and
along the western coast of South America beyond Valparaiso, perhaps
almost up to the frontier of Bolivia. Dr. Cunningham observed
both this species and *C. coscoroba* near Sandy Point in the Straits
of Magellan, where they were breeding.

In the Falkland Islands the Black-necked Swan is found throughout the year, but is rather scarce and very wild. It seldom breeds
on the main island, but retires to the adjacent islets for that pur-
pose. Dr. Burmeister mentions its occurrence on the Paraná, and
also states that it is found on the island of Santa Catharina off the
coast of Brazil, this being probably nearly its most northern
limit.

The Black-necked Swan has long been introduced into Europe ;
and seldom a year passes but one or more broods are reared in the
Gardens of this Society.

2. CYGNUS COSCOROBA.

Anas coscoroba, Mol. Stor. Nat. Chili, p. 207 ; Gm. S. N. i. p. 503
(1788) ex Molina.

Anser coscoroba, Vieill. Enc. Méth. p. 112 (1823).

Cygnus coscoroba, Hartl. Ind. Az. p. 27 ; Eyd. & Gerv. Ois. de
Favorite, in Mag. de Zool. 1836, p. 36 ; Gray and Mitch. Gen. of
Birds, t. clxvi. ; Gay, Faun. Chil. p. 446 (1848) (Chili) ; Burm. J.
für Orn. 1860, p. 226, et La Plata-Reise, ii. p. 512 (Paraná) ; P.
Z. S. 1872, p. 365 ; Scl. P. Z. S. 1867, pp. 334, 339 (Chili), 1860,
p. 388 (Falklands); Abbott, Ibis, 1861, p. 159 (Falklands); Schl.
Mus. des P.-B. Anseres, p. 83 ; Ph. & Landb. Cat. Av. Chil. p. 41 ;
Scl. & Salv. Ibis, 1869, p. 284 (Rio Galegos); Nomencl. p. 129.

Cygnus anatoides, King, P. Z. S. 1830-31, p. 15 (Straits of
Magellan) : Eyton, Mon. Anat. p. 101 (1838).

Cygnus chionis, Ill. in Mus. Berol. ; Licht. Nomencl. p. 101.

Coscoroba chionis, Bp. C. R. xliii. p. 648 (1856).

24*

Ganso blanco, Az. Ap. no. 436 (La Plata), undè
Anser candidus, Vieillot, N. D. xxiii. p. 331 (1816), et Enc.
Méth. p. 351 (1823).
Coscoroba candida, Reich. Nat. Syst. d. Vög. p. x.

*Albus; primariorum apicibus nigris; loris plumosis; rostro lato
anatiformi ruberrimo, ungue carneo; iride fere nigra; pedibus
rubro-carneis (ave viva) : long. tota circ. 40·0, alæ 17·5, caudæ
5·8, rostri a rictu 3·0, tarsi 3·5, dig. med. cum ungue 5·0*
(Descr. exempl. ex Chilia in Mus. S. & G.).

Hab. Chili (*Molina, Gay, Philippi & Landbeck*); Straits of Magellan (*King, Cunningham*); Falkland Islands (*Abbott*); Buenos
Ayres (*Azara, Burmeister*).

Burmeister observed the Coscoroba Swan in large numbers on the
rivers Paraná and Salado, especially in the lagoons bordering the
river near Santa Fé. During the winter, he says, it keeps in flocks
like our Swan. He also observed it at Mendoza and in the large
lakes of the Pampas.

Azara met with only two individuals of this species in Paraguay,
and a small flock at about 28° S. lat. He says, however, that
it abounds in enormous flocks in the lagoons bordering the La
Plata.

The Coscoroba Swan is rare in Chili, according to Philippi and
Landbeck, who, however, give no details respecting its range on the
western coast, though they mention a young one having been brought
to them from the Straits of Magellan.

Mare harbour is the only part of East Falkland where Capt. Abbott ever saw or heard of this species. At that spot there is usually
a flock of eight or ten to be seen. They breed in the neighbourhood,
young birds of about a month old having been observed.

Living specimens of this Swan were brought to England in
1870 and 1871, but as yet have not reproduced. A pair made a
nest in the Society's Gardens; and eggs were laid in 1872, but no
young birds were hatched.

Subfamily III. ANATINÆ.

Genus 1. DENDROCYGNA.   Type.

Dendronessa, Wagl. Isis, 1832, p. 281 (nec Sw.).. *D. arcuata.*
Dendrocygna, Sw. Class. Birds, ii. p. 365 (1837). *D. arcuata.*
Leptotarsis, Eyt. Mon. Anatinæ, p. 29 (1838) .. *D. eytoni.*

This genus is a good example of what may be called a Tropicopolitan group, being represented nearly everywhere within the tropics.
In America four very distinct species are found, besides another that
is scarcely more than a representative form.

1. DENDROCYGNA FULVA.

Penelope mexicana, Briss. vi. p. 390 (Mexico), undè
Anas fulva, Gm. S. N. i. p. 530 (1788); Vieill. Enc. Méth.
p. 136 (1823); Max. Beitr. iv. p. 918; Wagl. Isis, 1831, p. 532;

Burm. Syst. Ueb. iii. p. 435; *J. f. Orn.* 1860, p. 226 (Tucuman);
La Plata-Reise, ii. p. 514.

Dendrocygna fulva, Baird, Birds N. Am. p. 770, t. 63 (Fort Tejon,
Cal.) : Scl. P. Z. S. 1864, p. 301, and 1866, p. 149 ; Scl. & Salv.
P. Z. S. 1869, p. 635 (Buenos Ayres), et Nomencl. p. 129 ; Schl.
Mus. des P.-B. *Anseres*, p. 87 ; Pelz. Orn. Bras. p. 319 (1870);
Burm. P. Z. S. 1872, p. 377 (Buenos Ayres); Lawr. Mem. Bost.
Soc. N. H. ii. p. 313 (Mazatlan).

Anas virgata, Max. Reise, i. p. 322.

Pato roxo y negro, Az. Apunt. no. 436, unde

Anas bicolor, Vieill. N. D. v. p. 136 ; Enc. Méth. p. 356; Hartl.
Ind. Az. p. 28 ; Léot. Ois. Trin. p. 514 (1866) (Trinidad).

Anas sinuata, Licht. in Mus. Berol.

Anas collaris, Merrem, in Ersch. u. Grub. Enc. sect. i. vol. xxxv.
p. 31.

Dendrocygna major, Jerdon, Birds of Ind. iii. p. 790 (India);
Scl. P. Z. S. 1866, p. 148 (Madagascar).

*Castanea, pileo obscuriore, linea mediali colli postici nigra ; dorso
nigro, in parte anteriore castaneo transfasciato ; alis et cauda
nigris ; tectricibus alarum minoribus obscure badiis, tectricibus
supracaudalibus albis ; plumis hypochondriorum elongatis, castaneis, fascia mediali alba nigro utrinque marginata ornatis ;
rostro et pedibus nigris: long. tota 18·0, alæ 8·5, caudæ 2·0,
rostri a rictu 2·3, tarsi 2·0, dig. med. cum ungue 3·0 (Descr.
spec. ex Mexico, in Mus. S. & G.).*

Hab. Mexico (*Brisson, Grayson*); S.E. Brazil (*Max.*); Paraguay
and Buenos Ayres (*Azara, Burmeister*) ; Montevideo (*Sellow*).

Dendrocygna fulva, according to Burmeister, is found in the
eastern and northern districts of the La-Plata basin, on the rivers
Uruguay and Paraná, and as far north as Tucuman ; and Azara
observed it both in Paraguay and in Buenos Ayres.   In the Brazilian
empire it was obtained by Prince Maximilian on the river Belmonte
and also on the sea-coast near Porto Seguro ; but although Burmeister
states that it is found throughout Central Brazil, Natterer seems to
have failed to secure specimens.   It appears, so far as we know, to
be absent from the basin of the Amazons and from the whole of the
northern portion of the southern continent ; nor is it found in
Central America or in the West Indies.   In Mexico it reappears,
and would seem to be by no means rare, occurring from the Rio-
Grande frontier and California to Mazatlan and the valley of Mexico.
Singular as this distribution is, it is still more remarkable when we
consider that there appear to exist no tangible grounds for separating
the American bird from that called *D. major* by Jerdon, which
ranges throughout the peninsula of India and is also found in Madagascar !

2. DENDROCYGNA AUTUMNALIS.

Red-billed Whistling Duck, Edw. t. 194 (West Indies), unde
Anas autumnalis, Linn. S. N. i. p. 205 (1766).

Dendrocygna autumnalis, Eyton, Mon. Anat. p. 109 (1838);

Baird, B. of N. Am. p. 770 (1858) (Texas); Cassin, Pr. Ac. Phil.
1860, p. 197 (R. Truando); Scl. P. Z. S. 1858, p. 360; Scl. & Salv.
Ibis, 1859, p. 231; Taylor, Ibis, 1860, p. 315 (Lake Yojoa); Scl. &
Salv. P. Z. S. 1864, pp. 299 (partim) & 372 (Panamá), et Nomencl.
p. 129; Lawr. Ann. Lyc. N. Y. viii. p. 13 (Panamá), et ix. p. 143
(Costa Rica); Mem. Bost. Soc. N. H. ii. p. 313 (Mazatlan); Salv.
Ibis, 1865, p. 193.

*Capitis lateribus et gutture cinereis, hoc albicantiore, colli postici
lineu mediali brunnescenti-nigra ; pileo (versus nucham obscuriore), collo inferiore et corpore toto antico cum dorso medio et
scapularibus læte castaneo-brunneis, pectore paullo dilutiore ;
dorso postico, ventre toto et cauda nigris, ventre imo et tibiis
albo variegatis, crisso fere albo ; alis nigris, tectricibus alarum
minoribus internis ochracescentibus, mediis canis, externis albis ;
remigibus (extimo excepto) in pogonio externo et remigum tectricibus lactescenti-albidis ; rostro rubro, ungue nigro ; pedibus
flavis : long. tota 16·0, alæ 8·5, caudæ 2·8, tarsi 2·0, dig. med.
cum ungue 2·6, rostri a rictu 2·0 (Descr. maris ex Panama in
Mus. S. & G.).*

Hab. Mexico (*Grayson*); Guatemala (*Salvin*); Honduras (*Taylor*); Costa Rica (*Arcé*); Panama (*M'Leannan*).

Latham's description of his *Anas autumnalis* was based upon
Edwards's plate 194 ; and upon reference to this figure we feel no
doubt that a specimen of the Central-American form of this Duck
was the subject of Edwards's drawing. Moreover Edwards says, in
the text of his work, that his specimen was brought from the West
Indies.

The birds described by Baird from the Rio Grande, on the Texan
frontier, evidently agree with Central-American examples ; but Baird
seems to have had specimens of the South-American form also before
him when writing his notes on this species in the 'Birds of North
America.' He attributes the greyness of the lower neck and breast
in a South-American specimen to greater maturity—a view which can
hardly be maintained, seeing that this peculiarity is found, so far as
our experience goes, *only* in examples from the southern part of
America.

In Central America this species is only found in the hottest part
of the country and in the lagoons near the sea-coast, especially in
those which lie in such abundance along the Pacific coast of Guatemala. During Salvin's stay there in 1863 he not unfrequently saw
small flocks of this Duck, and also obtained specimens. In Honduras
Mr. Taylor found this Tree-Duck abundant on Lake Yojoa. From
Costa Rica we have an example collected by Arcé on the Gulf of
Nicoya ; and at Panama, whence we also have a specimen, it is not
uncommon. M'Leannan had a pair of this species alive when Salvin
stayed at his Station at Lion Hill.

The bird found on the Truando by Lieut. Michler's party probably
belongs to this race ; but we cannot speak with certainty on this
point. It may also extend its range along the west coast as far as

Guayaquil ; but this, too, remains to be determined ; nor can its eastward limit be as yet defined. The form found in Trinidad (as described by Léotaud) certainly belongs to the next species.

3. DENDROCYGNA DISCOLOR.

Dendrocygna autumnalis, Cab. in Schomb. Guian. iii. p. 762 ; Scl. P. Z. S. 1864, p. 299 (partim) ; Scl. & Salv. P. Z. S. 1866, p. 200 (Ucayali); Léot. Ois. Trin. p. 507 (1866) (Trinidad); Schl. Mus. des P.-B. *Anseres,* p. 92 ; Pelz. Orn. Bras. p. 320 (1870) ; Finsch, P. Z. S. 1870, p. 589 (Trinidad).

Canard Siffleur de Cayenne, Buff. Pl. Enl. 826.

Dendrocygna discolor, Scl. & Salv. Nomencl. p. 161 (1873).

Capite, collo antico, pectore et dorso superiore griseis, pileo obscuriore ; gutture albicante, torque colli inferi indistincte castaneo ; dorso medio læte castaneo ; ventre, alis et cauda nigris ; tectricibus alarum minoribus internis ochracescentibus, mediis canis, externis albis ; remigibus (extimo excepto) in pogonio externo et remigum tectricibus albis ; crisso albo nigroque vario, rostro rubro, ungue nigro ; pedibus flavis : long. tota 16·0, alæ 8·0, caudæ 2·5, rostri a rictu 2·2, tarsi 2·0, dig. med. cum ungue 2·5 (Descr. exmpl. ex Surinam in Mus. S. & G.).

Hab. Columbia, S. Martha (*Deppe, in Mus. Berol.*); Surinam (*Kappler*); Trinidad (*Léotaud*); Guiana (*Schomb.*) ; Cayenne (*Buffon*); Ucayali (*Burtlett*); Barra do Rio Negro, and Minas Geraes (*Natterer*).

Obs. Similis præcedenti, sed dorso superiore et pectore canis nec castaneis.

This southern form of *D. autumnalis* is distinguishable at a glance from that of Central America by the upper portion of the back being of a different colour from the middle and lower back—the former being of a grey tint, the latter rich chestnut-brown. In the northern form no such difference is apparent, the whole upper surface being of the same chestnut tint. The breast in the former bird also is greyish, and in the latter chestnut.

D. discolor, as we have proposed to term it, is found in the northern part of South America, extending from the littoral of Columbia and Guiana over the great Amazon valley, and occasionally ranging as far south as Mato Grosso and the interior of Minas Geraes, where specimens were obtained by Natterer.

4. DENDROCYGNA ARBOREA.

Anas arborea, Linn. S. N. i. p. 207 (1766); Gm. S. N. i. p. 540 (1788); Vieill. Enc. Méth. p. 141 (1823).

Dendrocygna arborea, Eyton, Mon. Anat. p. 110 (1838); Gosse, B. Jam. p. 395 (Jamaica); Cab. J. f. Orn. 1857, p. 227 (Cuba); Thienem. J. f. Orn. 1857, p. 157 (Cuba); A. & E. Newton, Ibis, 1859, p. 366 (St. Croix); Scl. P. Z. S. 1864, p. 300 ; March, Pr. Ac. Phil. 1864, p. 70 (Jamaica); Gundl. Repert. F.-N. i. p. 387

(1866) et J. für Orn. 1875, p. 375 (Cuba) ; Bryant, Pr. Bost. Soc.
N. H. xi. (1866) p. 70 (Inagua) ; Schl. Mus. des P.-B. *Anseres*,
p. 84 ; Scl. & Salv. Nomencl. p. 73.
Black-billed Whistling Duck, Edw. Glean. t. 193.
Canard Siffleur de la Jamaïque, Buff. Pl. Enl. 804.
Anas jacquini, Gm. S. N. i. p. 536, ex Jacquin, Beitr. p. 5.
n. 3 (?).

*Fusco-brunnea, capite ochracescentiore, nucha cum stria colli postici
nigra, torque collari nigro variegata ; dorsi plumis et tectricibus alarum marginibus pallidioribus ornatis, his quoque nigro
maculatis ; subtus gutture toto albo, pectore fulvescente, abdomine, præcipue in hypochondriis, albo nigroque variegato ; dorso
postico et cauda nigris ; alis cinereis, remigibus fusco terminatis ; rostro et pedibus nigris : long. tota* 18·5, *candæ* 3·0,
rostri a rictu 2·2, *tarsi* 2·5, *dig. med. cum ungue* 2·8 (Descr.
exempl. ex Jamaica in Mus. Brit.).

Hab. Cuba (*Gundlach*) ; Jamaica (*Gosse, March*) ; St. Croix
(*Newton fr.*).

This Tree-duck is a resident in Cuba, where, according to Dr. Gundlach, it is common. It is said to rest during the day and to visit the
lagoons towards dusk. It nests from June to September. Mr. March
remarks that is a permanent resident in Jamaica, frequenting the
lagoons and morasses where mangroves abound, and feeding by night
as well as by day. The habits of this species in Jamaica are also
fully described by Mr. Gosse (*l. c.*). Numerous flocks frequent the
millet-fields in Jamaica from December to the end of February. They
are described as beating down the corn as they descend in compact
flocks, and then picking the grain from the ears trampled under foot,
which they cannot otherwise reach as it stands erect. In this manner
they do a considerable amount of damage. The species is easily tamed,
but does not appear to breed in confinement.

In St. Croix the Messrs. Newton state that the " Mangrove-
Duck " is pretty common ; but they are unable to say for certain
whether it breeds in the island. It is more often heard than seen,
its habit being to resort to its feeding-ground at night and to rest
during the day in the recesses of the mangrove-swamps.

5. DENDROCYGNA VIDUATA.

Anas viduata, Linn. S. N. i. p. 205 (1766) ; Jacquin, Beitr. i. p. 3,
t. i. ; Gm. S. N. i. p. 536 (1788) (Cartagena) ; Vieill. Enc. Méth.
p. 132 (1823) ; Max. Beitr. iv. p. 921 (Brazil) ; Burm. Syst. Ueb. iii.
p. 434.
Dendrocygna viduata, Eyton, Mon. Anat. p. 110 (1838) ; Cab. in
Schomb. Guiana, iii. p. 762 ; Hartl. Ind. Az. p. 28 ; Tsch. F.P. p. 54 ;
D'Orb. Voy. i. p. 448 ; Burm. La Plata-Reise, ii. p. 515 (Tucuman) ;
J. f. Orn. 1860, p. 266 ; Gundl. Repert. F.-N. i. p. 388, J. für Orn.
1875, p. 377 (Cuba) ; Scl. P. Z. S. 1864, p. 299 ; Léot. Ois. Trin.
p. 509 (1866) (Trinidad) ; Scl. & Salv. P. Z. S. 1866, p. 200 (Ucayali), 1869, p. 160 (Rep. Arg.), et Nomencl. p. 129 ; Schl. Mus. des

P.-B. *Anseres*, p. 90; Pelz. Orn. Bras. p. 319 (1870); Reinh. Fugl.
Bras. Camp. p. 21 (1870) (Lagoa Santa).
Canard du Marugnon, Buff. Pl. Enl. 808.
Pato cara blanca, Az. Apunt. no. 435.

*Facie tota et macula gutturali albis ; uucha, collo antico, abdo-
mine medio, cauda, dorso postico et alis nigris ; collo postico et
humeris castaneis ; dorso medio et scapularibus brunneis, plumis
singulis ochraceo marginatis; tectricibus alarum olivaceo-nigris ;
hypochondriis albo nigroque transfasciatis : rostro et pedibus
nigris : long. tota 17·0, alæ 9·0, caudæ 2·5, tarsi 2·0, dig. med.
cum ungue 2·6, rostri a rictu 2·2 (Descr. exempl. ex Columbia in
Mus. S. & G.).*

Hab. Columbia (*Mus. S. & G.*); Guiana (*Schomb.*); Rio Brancho
(*Natt.*); Trinidad (*Léotaud*); Upper Amazons (*Bartlett*); Peru
(*Tschudi*); Bolivia (*D'Orbigny*); Paraguay (*Azara*); Tucuman (*Bur-
meister*); Brazil (*Maximilian*); Rio Paraná and Cuyaba (*Natterer*);
Lagoa Santa (*Lund*); Bahia (*Wucherer*); Cuba (*Gundlach*).

This species has a very wide range in South America ; but though
its casual appearance in Cuba has been recorded, it has never yet been
met with in Central America. Commencing from the valley of the
Magdalena it spreads over the whole continent, including the island
of Trinidad, as far as the vicinity of Buenos Ayres. In Paraguay,
Azara saw it in large flocks of as many as two hundred individuals
and more. He notes its cry as "*bi-bi-bi*," which is uttered as it flies
at all hours of the night. The members of a flock fly in a straight line
or crescent.

Genus 2. SARCIDIORNIS. Type.
Sarcidiornis, Eyton, Mon. Anat. p. 20 (1838) .. *S. melanonota.*

This genus appears to be truly Tropicopolitan, and is represented
by two or three species or closely allied forms in India, Africa, and
America.

SARCIDIORNIS CARUNCULATA.

"*Anas carunculata*, Ill.," Licht. Abh. Ak. Berlin, 1816-17, p. 176.
El Pato crestudo, Az. Apunt. no. 438.
Pato de crista, Max. Beitr. iii. p. 942.
Anser melanotus, Burm. Syst. Ueb. iii. p. 434.
Sarcidiornis regia, Hartl. Ind. Az. p. 27 (1847); Burm. La Plata-
Reise, ii. p. 513 (Tucuman); J. f. Orn. 1860, p. 266; Scl. P. Z. S.
1867, p. 339, 1868, p. 532; Pelz. Orn. Bras. p. 319; Scl. & Salv.
Nomencl. p. 129.

Hab. Paraguay (*Azara*); Tucuman (*Burmeister*); interior of
prov. Bahia (*Maximilian*); Matogrosso and Barra do Rio Negro
(*Natterer*).

We are unable to give a description of this species, as no authentic
South-American examples are at present accessible to us. It is
therefore not possible for us to give independent testimony as to the
identity or distinctness of the birds found in South America, Africa,
and India ; but we have good reason to believe that the South-
American form is really separable.

Hartlaub (*l. s. c.*) says there is no sufficient difference between American and Indian specimens; but v. Pelzeln distinguishes the American form from the African and Indian birds by its darker flanks.

The South-American bird has, as will be seen from the above quotations, usually been identified with the Pato Real, or *Anas regia* of Molina; but we now know that the *Sarcidiornis* does not occur at all in Chili, and that the "Pato Real" of that country is *Mareca chiloensis*, according to Philippi and Landbeck (Cat. Av. Chil. p. 95), though Molina's vague description may have had some reference to *Cairina moschata*. If, then, as would appear to be the case, the American bird is really separable from the Indian, the proper name for this species is *carunculata*—a term based by Illiger on Azara's *Pato crestudo*, and published by Lichtenstein in 1818.

The range of this Duck in South America is by no means extended; and it has seldom been noticed beyond the upper waters of the basin of the Paraná. It occurs, however, in the interior of Bahia, according to Prince Maximilian; and Natterer met with it at Barra do Rio Negro, on the Amazons, in July 1832.

Genus 3. CAIRINA.

Cairina, Fleming, Phil. of Zool. p. 260 (1822).
Moschatus, Less. Ind. Orn. i. p. 633 (1831).
Gymnathus, Nuttall, Man. Orn. ii. p. 403 (1834).

This genus contains a single form, originally American, but now introduced into the Old World and naturalized in many parts of the tropics.

CAIRINA MOSCHATA.

Anas moschata, Linn. S. N. i. p. 199; Max. Beitr. iv. p. 910 (Brazil); Schl. Mus. des P.-B. *Anseres*, p. 73.
Cairina moschata, Cab. in Schomb. Guiana, iii. p. 763; Tsch. F. P. p. 54; D'Orb. Voy. i. p. 111; Burm. Syst. Ueb. iii. p. 440 (Brazil), et La Plata-Reise, ii. p. 514 (Paraná and Tucuman); J. f. Orn. 1860, p. 266; Moore, P. Z. S. 1859, p. 65 (Honduras); Scl. & Salv. Ibis, 1859, p. 232 (Guatemala); P. Z. S. 1864, p. 373 (Panama), 1866, p. 200 (Ucayali), 1867, p. 979 (Pebas); Salv. Ibis, 1865, p. 198; Taylor, Ibis, 1860, p. 315 (Honduras); Léot. Ois. Trin. p. 521 (1866) (Trinidad); Pelz. Orn. Bras. p. 320 (1870); Reinh. Fugl. Bras. Camp. p. 21 (1870) (Lagoa Santa); Lawr. Mem. Bost. Soc. N. H. ii. p. 315 (Mazatlan).
Carina moschata, Eyton, Mon. Anat. p. 142 (1838).
Cairina sylvestris, Stephens, Zool. xiii. p. 69.
Anas marianæ, Shaw, Nat. Misc. ii. t. 69 (!).
El Pato Grande o Real, Az. Apunt. no. 437.
Le Canard musqué, Buff. Pl. Enl. 986.

Capite toto, collo, et corpore subtus brunneo-nigris, abdomine lineis albis angustissimis transvittato; dorso iridescente purpureo, plumis singulis nigro marginatis, scapularibus et tertiariis elongatis cum cauda lœte viridi-nitentibus; secundariis chalybeo-cæruleo indutis; primariis nigris; tectricibus alarum omnibus supra et subtus cum plumis axillaribus pure albis; hypochondriis viridi vix tinctis; rostri carunculis rubris, pedibus nigris: long. tota 29·0, *alæ* 15·0, *caudæ* 7·5, *rostri a rictu* 2·6, *torsi* 2·3, *dig. med. cum ungue* 3·8 (Descr. maris ex Guatemala, in Mus. S. & G.). Fem. *mari similis sed minor: long. tota* 25·0, *alæ* 12·5, *caudæ* 5·5, *rostri a rictu* 2·3, tarsi 1·8, *dig. med. cum ungue* 2·9.

Hab. Paraguay (*Azara*); Paraná and Tucuman (*Burmeister*); Lagoa Santa (*Reinhardt*); Bolivia (*D'Orbigny*); Peru (*Tschudi*); Brazil (*Maximilian, Burmeister*); Amazonia (*Bartlett, Hauxwell*); Guiana (*Schomburgk*); Trinidad (*Léotaud*); Panama (*M'Leannan*); Honduras (*Taylor*); Guatemala (*Salvin*); Mexico (*Grayson, Xantus*).

The Muscovy Duck, so well known in a domestic state nearly all over the world, is a native of the hottest portion of tropical America. It is usually found in lowland swampy districts; and where there are extensive forests it not unfrequently abounds. During the day the birds remain in the forest-swamps; but towards evening numbers may be seen sitting on the lower boughs of trees standing on the margin of a clearing.

In Guatemala, Salvin found this Duck abundant on the Pacific coast in lagoons near Santana Mixtan and also at Huamuchal. It is likewise met with on the Atlantic side on the Rio Polochic, and also between Lake Peten and Lake Yax-ha. Its extreme northern limit seems to be N.W. Mexico, where Col. Grayson found it at Mazatlan, and Xantus at Rio Zacatula.

Its southern range extends to the upper Paraná and Tucuman. It is not uncommon in Paraguay, according to Azara, although not found on the La Plata. It is to be seen usually in pairs or singly, but also in flocks of twenty or thirty. It always roosts in trees, usually resorting to the same trees night after night. The nest, in which from ten to fourteen eggs are deposited, is made in a hole or fork of a large tree at some elevation from the ground. It seeks its food not only in the rivers, but on moonlight nights resorts to the maize and cornfields and also plucks up the roots of mandioca.

The native habitat of the Muscovy Duck was known to some of the earliest writers. The date of its introduction as a domesticated species into Europe and elsewhere does not appear to have been recorded, but doubtless dates back to soon after the Spanish conquests in America.

Genus 4. ANAS.   Type.

Anas, Linn. S. N. i. p. 194 (1766)............. *A. boschas.*
Boschas, Sw. Class. B. ii. p. 367 (1857) .... *A. boschas.*
Chauliodus, Sw. Faun. Bor.-Amer. p. 440 (1831) *A. strepera.*
Ktinorhynchus, Eyton, Mon. Anat. p. 137 (1838) *A. strepera.*
Chaulelasmus, G. R. Gray; Pr. Bonap. Geog. Comp.
List of B. p. 58 (1838) .... *A. strepera.*

Five species of true *Anas* (or, at least, not yet separated from the

Linnean type) occur within the Neotropical Region. Three of them
are stray visitors from the north into the Antilles ; the remaining
two are peculiar Antarctic species.

1. ANAS BOSCHAS.

Anas boschas, Linn. S. N. i. p. 205 (1766) ; Baird, B. of N. Am.
p. 774 ; Cab. J. f. Orn. 1857, p. 229 (Cuba) ; March, Pr. Ac. Phil.
1864, p. 72 (Jamaica) ; Gundl. Repert. F.-N. i. p. 388, et J. für
Orn. 1875, p. 378 (Cuba) ; Scl. & Salv. Nomencl. p. 129 ; Lawr.
Ann. Lyc. N. Y. viii. p. 13 (Panama) et Mem. Bost. Soc. N. H. ii.
p. 311 (Mexico).

Anas maxima, Scl. P. Z. S. 1859, p. 370 (Mexico).

Hab. Cuba (*Gundlach*) ; Jamaica (*March*) ; Mexico (*De Oca*,
Grayson) ; Panama (*M'Leannan*).

According to Dr. Gundlach, *A. boschas* is rarely seen wild in
Cuba ; but in 1850 a flock on passage from the north settled in the
lagoons near Cardenas, and the bird is occasionally to be seen in
the market of Havana. Mr. March says it is rare in Jamaica. In
Central America it has been recorded from Mexico and Panama, but
nowhere else.

2. ANAS OBSCURA.

Anas obscura, Gm. S. N. i. p. 541 (1788) ; Baird, B. of N. Am.
p. 775 ; Cab. J. f. Orn. 1857, p. 229 (Cuba); March, Pr. Ac. Phil.
1864, p. 72 (Jamaica); Scl. & Salv. Nomencl. p. 129 ; Lawr. Mem.
Bost. Soc. N. H. ii. p. 314 (Mexico).

Hab. Jamaica (*March*) ; Tepic, Mexico (*Grayson*).

The Dusky Duck is said to be of rare occurrence in Jamaica. In
Cuba, Dr. Gundlach formerly suspected its occasional presence, but
does not mention it in his last ' Revista de las Aves Cubanas.' In
Mexico it has hitherto only been noticed at Tepic by Grayson.

3. ANAS SPECULARIS.

Anas specularis, King, Zool. Journ. iv. p. 98 (1828) ; Eyton,
Mon. Anat. p. 138 (1838) ; Jard. & Selb. Ill. Orn. iv. tab. 40 ;
Gay, Faun. Chil. p. 450 ; Cassin, Gilliss's Exp. ii. p. 202 ; Scl.
P. Z. S. 1867, p. 335 (Chili) ; Ph. & Landb. Cat. Av. Chil. p. 42 ;
Scl. & Salv. Nomencl. p. 129.

Anas chalcoptera, Kittlitz, Mém. prés. Acad. St. Pétersb. ii. p. 471,
t. 5 (1835) ; Schl. Mus. des P.-B., *Anseres*, p. 46 ; Gray, Hand-l.
iii. p. 82.

Supra chalybeio-nigra, cervice postica et uropygio fumoso-brunneis;
dorsi superioris plumis hoc colore marginatis ; capite toto et
nucha nigris, plaga magna faciali utrinque et gutture medio in
semitorquem collarem transeunte distinctissime albis ; subtus
valde dilutior et rufescentior, et fasciis transversis rufis in pectore variegata ; alis et interscapulio chalybeio-nigris ; speculo
alari lato viride cupreo, hujus parte distali velutino-nigra
margine albo terminata ; hypochondriis aeneo-nigro maculatis ;

plumis axillaribus albis; rostro obscuro, pedibus flavis: long. tota 21·0, alæ 11·0, caudæ 4·8, tarsi 1·9, rostri a rictu 2·3.

Fem. *mari similis, sed coloribus minus claris.*

Hab. Magellan Straits (*King*); Southern and Central Chili (*Phil. & Landb.*).

This Duck is very remarkable for its conspicuous white patch on each side of the face and pure white throat and neck, as well as the large richly coloured alar speculum. So far as we yet know, it is exclusively a western species. According to Philippi and Landbeck it is common from the Straits of Magellan as far north as Valdivia, but is rare in the central provinces of Chili.

4. Anas cristata.

Crested Duck, Lath. Syn. iii. p. 513, undè

Anas cristata, Gm. S. N. i. p. 540 (1788) (Statenland); Gay, Faun. Chil. p. 449 (1848); Gould, P. Z. S. 1859, p. 96 (Falklands); Scl. P. Z. S. 1860, p. 389 (Falklands), 1867, p. 335 (Chili); Abbott, Ibis, 1861, p. 160 (Falklands); Ph. & Landb. Cat. Av. Chil. p. 41; Scl. & Salv. P. Z. S. 1867, p. 990 (Salinas, Peru); Ibis, 1870, p. 499 ('Tuesday Bay'), et Nomencl. p. 129; Schl. Mus. des P.-B. *Anseres*, p. 39.

Anas specularoides, King, Zool. Journ. iv. p. 98 (1838).

Anas pyrrhogaster, Meyen, Nov. Act. xvi. Suppl. p. 119, t. xxv. (Maipu, Chili).

Dafila pyrrhogaster, Eyton, Mon. Anat. p. 113 (1838).

Supra terreno-fusca, colore pallidiore in dorso superiore variegata; pileo fuscescenti-nigro in cristam elongatam desinente; speculo alari lato cupreo-viridi, parte distali nigra, fascia externa alba terminata; subtus fusca, magis rufescens et maculis indistinctis in pectore notata; crisso et subalaribus fere nigris, harum plaga media alba; rostri maxilla nigra, mandibula flava, pedibus nigris: long. tota 20·0, alæ 10·5, caudæ 5·0, rostri a rictu 2·1, tarsi 1·8, dig. med. cum ungue 2·4.

Hab. Falklands (*Abbott*); Magellan Straits (*Cunn.*); Chili (*Ph. & Landb.*); S. Peru (*Whitely*).

This species has a wider range than the last, extending northwards into Southern Peru, where Mr. Whitely obtained specimens in 1867 at Salinas, a salt lake on the Cordillera, above Arequipa, at an altitude of 14,000 feet. In Chili, Philippi and Landbeck tell us, it inhabits the high cordilleras in summer, but descends during winter to the plains, and is found along the coast down to the Magellan Straits, where Dr. Cunningham obtained specimens.

The Crested Duck is common everywhere on the Falkland islands, mostly frequenting salt water, though occasionally seen near freshwater pools. Old birds are always found in pairs. They live upon shellfish. They retire inland to breed; and the duck lays five eggs, in a nest covered with down. The eggs are laid from the beginning of October to the beginning of November.

The only near ally of this Duck in the Neotropical region is the preceding species, from which it may be at once distinguished by the

382   MESSRS. SCLATER AND SALVIN ON   [Apr. 4,

absence of the conspicuous white face-markings and the small crest.
It is, no doubt, the *Anas specularoides* of King.

5. ANAS STREPERA.

Anas strepera, Linn. S. N. i. p. 100 (1766): Scl. & Salv. Nomencl.
p. 129.
   Chaulelasmus streperus, Baird, B. of N. Amer. p. 782 : March,
Pr. Ac. Phil. 1864, p. 72 (Jamaica) ; Gundl. Repert. F.-N. i. p. 389,
et J. für Orn. 1875, p. 381 (Cuba) ; Lawr. Mem. Bost. Soc. N. H.
ii. p. 315 (Mexico).
   Hab. Cuba (*Gundl.*) ; Jamaica (*March*) ; Mexico (*Grayson*).
   The occurrence of a single male bird of this species in the market
of Havana is the sole authority for its admission into the list of Cuban
birds. In Jamaica, however, Mr. March says, it is sometimes abundant, but of irregular occurrence. Its presence in Mexico is confined
to the N.W. provinces, where Grayson observed it.

Genus 5. HETERONETTA.   Type.
Heteronetta, Salvadori, Atti de la Soc. Ital. d.
Sci. Nat. viii. p. 574 (1865) .... *H. melanocephala*.
   This is certainly an aberrant form of *Anas* in many respects; and
Dr. Salvadori is probably correct in isolating it.   Schlegel even goes
so far as to put it with the *Fuligulæ* ; but before accepting this view,
we require a knowledge of its tracheal formation.

HETERONETTA MELANOCEPHALA.

Pato cabeza negra, Az. Apunt. no. 438 (Buenos Ayres), undè
Anas melanocephala, Vieill. N. D. v. p. 163 (1816), et Enc. Méth.
p. 354 (1823); Hartl. Ind. Az. p. 28 ; Cassin, Gilliss's Exp. ii.
p. 202, t. xxv. (1856); Scl. P. Z. S. 1867, p. 335 (Chili) ; Phil. &
Landb. Cat. Av. Chil. p. 42 ; Scl. & Salv. Nomencl. p. 129.
   Heteronetta melanocephala, Salvad. Atti Soc. Ital. viii. p. 374
(1866).
   Fuligula melanocephala, Schl. Mus. des P.-B. *Anseres*, p. 32.
   Anas nigriceps, Licht. in Mus. Berol. ; Nomencl. p. 101.
   Anas atricapilla, Merrem, in Ersch. u. Grub. Enc. sect. i. vol. xxxv.
p. 26.
   *Supra saturate nigricanti-fusca, rufescente minutissime vermicu-
lata ; capite colloque toto fuliginose nigris ; secundariorum
fascia terminali angusta alba ; subtus sordide alba, in pectore
summo hypochondriis et crisso rufescente irrorata ; rostro nigricante, macula basali utrinque carnea ; pedibus corneis : long.
tota 14·5, alæ 6·3, caudæ 2·3, tarsi 1·1, rostri a rictu 2·0.
Fem. pileo dorso concolori, genis fuscis nigro vermiculatis, gula
et stria superciliari indistincta albidis diversa.*
   Hab. Buenos Ayres (*Azara*): Chili prov. of Santiago (*Ph. &
Landb.*); Brazil, Rio Grande do Sul (*Max.*); Mendoza (*Weisshaupt*).
   This peculiar Duck was first described by Azara, who " bought a
pair in Buenos Ayres," where, however, Burmeister does not seem to

have recognized it.　Prince Maximilian tells us (Beitr. iv. p. 932) that
he has received examples from Rio Grande do Sul ; and Weisshaupt
obtained a series of skins during his excursion from Santiago to
Mendoza, some of which are in Salvin and Godman's collection.

In Chili, where it also occurs, Philippi and Landbeck say that up
to the present time this species has not been found beyond the province of Santiago, and that the hunters confound it with *Erismatura
ferruginea*.

Genus 6. QUERQUEDULA.　　　Type.

Querquedula, Steph. Gen. Zool. xii. p. 142 (1824) .. *Q. circia*.
Nettion, Kaup, Nat. Syst. p. 95 (1829) .... *Q. crecca*.
Cyanopterus, Eyton, Mon. Anat. p. 130 (1838) .... *Q. circia*.
Pterocyanea, Bp. Cat. Met. Ucc. Eur. p. 71 (1842).. *Q. circia*.

Ten *Querquedulæ* (under which head we embrace the Teals and
Garganeys) occur within the Neotropical region.　Of these, two are
northern species, which visit the Antilles and Central America in
winter ; the remaining eight are endemic Neotropical species, one of
which, however, has extended its northern range into the southern
portion of the Nearctic region.

The ten Neotropical *Querquedulæ* may be diagnosed as follows :—

a. Tectricibus alar. min. cœruleis.
　Plaga faciei utrinque alba...................................... 1. *discors*.
　Facie (cum corpore antico) rubra .... 2. *cyanoptera*.
b. Tectricibus alar. min. fuscis.
　b'. Pileo et cervicis lateribus in mare rubris .... 3. *carolinensis*.
　c'. Pileo et cervicis lateribus nigro fasciolatis.
　　c". Rostro sup. ad basin flavo.
　　　Major : interscapulio dorso fere concolori............... 4. *oxyptera*.
　　　Minor : interscapulio nigro variegato.................... 5. *flavirostris*.
　　d". Rostro toto nigro .... 6. *andium*.
　d'. Pileo fuscescenti-nigro ; cervicis lateribus albis.
　　Rostro superiore ad basin rubro .... 7. *versicolor*.
　　Rostro toto nigro .... 8. *puna*.
c. Tectricibus alar. min. nigris.
　Pileo nigro.. 9. *torquata*.
　Pileo fusco .... 10. *brasiliensis*.

1. QUERQUEDULA DISCORS.

Anas discors, Linn. S. N. i. p. 205 (1766).

Querquedula discors, Steph. Gen. Zool. xii. p. 149 ; Baird, B. of
N. Am. p. 779 ; Cab. J. f. Orn. 1857, p. 228 (Cuba) ; Sallé, P. Z. S.
1857, p. 237 (S. Domingo) ; Scl. P. Z. S. 1857, p. 206 (Jalapa,
Mexico), 1859, p. 393, 1860, p. 254 (Mexico) ; Scl. & Salv. Ibis,
1859, p. 231 (Guatemala), et Nomencl. p. 129 ; Salv. Ibis, 1865,
p. 193 ; Gundl. Repert. F.-N. i. p. 389, et J. für Orn. 1875, p. 380
(Cuba) ; March, Pr. Acad. Phil. 1864, p. 71 (Jamaica) ; Lawr. Ann.
Lyc. N. Y. viii. p. 101 (Sombrero), ix. (1868) p. 143 (Costa Rica) ;
Mem. Bost. Soc. N. H. ii. p. 314 (Mexico) ; Bryant, Pr. Bost.
Soc. N. H. xi. p. 97 (S. Domingo) ; Salvin, P. Z. S. 1870, p. 219
(Veragua).

Pterocyanea discors, Léot. Ois. Trin. p. 516 (Trinidad).
Cyanopterus discors, Tayl. Ibis, 1860, p. 315 (Honduras).
Hab. Cuba (*Gundl.*); Jamaica (*March*); St. Domingo (*Sallé*, *Bryant*); Sombrero (*Lawr.*); Trinidad (*Léotaud*); Mexico, Jalapa and Orizaba (*Sallé*); Mazatlan (*Grayson*); Guatemala (*Salvin*); Honduras (*Taylor*); Costa Rica (*Lawrence*).

In Cuba this is the commonest of the North-American migratory Ducks, arriving about the beginning of September and leaving the island again in April. In Jamaica Mr. March says he has never seen the "Bluewings" earlier than November, and that they again appear in full summer-plumage in March and April on their way to the north. This species is likewise met with in the other Antilles, as far down as Trinidad.

On the continent, *Q. discors* has been traced down as far as Veragua, as will be seen by our list of localities. In Guatemala, Salvin found it common in winter, arriving in September and leaving again in March and April. It is met with in the high and low districts alike, chiefly on the lakes.

2. QUERQUEDULA CYANOPTERA.

Pato alas azulas, Az. Apunt. no. 434 (La Plata, Buenos Ayres), undè
Anas cyanoptera, Vieill. N. D. v. p. 104 (1816), et Enc. Méth. p. 352 (1823); Merrem, in Ersch. & Grub. Enc. sect. i. vol. xxxv. p. 33; Burm. J. f. Orn. 1860, p. 226; La Plata-Reise, ii. p. 516 (Mendoza); Schl. Mus. des P.-B. *Anseres*, p. 51.
Querquedula cyanoptera, Cass. Ill. Orn. p. 84, t. xv. (Louisiana, Utah), et Gilliss's Exp. ii. p. 202 (1856); Baird, B. of N. Amer. p. 780; Scl. P.Z.S. 1855, p. 164 (Bogotá, St. Martha), 1856, p. 310 (Mexico), 1860, p. 389 (Falklands), 1867, p. 355 (Chili); Gould, P.Z.S. 1859, p. 96 (Falklands); Abbott, Ibis, 1861, p. 161 (Falklands); Scl. & Salv. P.Z.S. 1869, p. 160 (Buenos Ayres), et Ibis, 1868, p. 189 (Sandy Point).
Anas cæruleata, Licht. in Mus. Berol.; Bibra, Denkschr. Ak. Wien, v. p. 131 (1853) (Chili); cf. J. f. Orn. 1855, p. 57; Lawr. Ann. Lyc. N.Y. v. p. 220 (California).
Querquedula cæruleata, Gay, Faun. Chil. p. 452 (1848); Ph. & Landb. Cat. Av. Chil. p. 42.
Pterocyanea cæruleata, Hartl. Ind. Az. p. 27 (1847).
Anas rafflesi, King, Zool. Journ. iv. p. 97 (1828); Jard. & Selb. Ill. Orn. t. 23.
Cyanopterus rafflesi, Eyton, Mon. Anat. p. 132 (1838).

Rubra, pileo nigro; interscapulio et scapularibus nigro variegatis; dorso postico nigricante; alarum tectricibus minoribus cæruleis; speculo alari viridi, fascia alba supra marginato; remigibus primariis nigris, secundariorum scapis albo et ochraceo flammulatis; rostro nigro, pedibus flavis: long. tota 18·0, alæ 7·6, caudæ 3·0, tarsi 1·3. Fem. supra nigricans, plumarum marginibus albidis; subtus sordide alba, fusco variegata, gutture albo nigro punctulato; alarum tectricibus et speculo sicut in mari.

Hab. Andes of Columbia (*Mus. S. G.*) ; St. Martha (*Verreaux*); Chili (*Ph. & Landb.*) ; Buenos Ayres (*Azara & Burm.*) ; Magellan Straits (*Cunningh.*) ; Falklands (*Abbott*).

This Duck, first discovered by Azara, has a very wide range in the New World, from the extreme south up to California on the west, and occurs accidentally in Louisiania. It was found by Azara only in the Rio de la Plata and Buenos Ayres ; but Burmeister observed it at Mendoza and on the Paraná, in lagoons and rivers. Philippi and Landbeck say that it is frequently met with throughout the republic of Chili ; and Dr. Cunningham obtained specimens in the Straits of Magellan. It seems not to be very common in East Falkland, though Capt. Abbott shot seven in one day at Mare Harbour. But it most probably breeds in these islands, as pairs were observed throughout the summer months.

In the eastern part of South America (that is, in Brazil, Amazonia, and Guiana) we do not find the occurrence of this Duck noticed ; but it is certainly met with in the Andes of Columbia and on the northern littoral of Venezuela, and probably keeps to the line of the Andes. It has not yet been recorded from any part of Central America ; but will probably be ultimately found there, as it is not un-common in the Western United States and has occurred accidentally in Louisiana.

3. QUERQUEDULA CAROLINENSIS.

Anas carolinensis, Gm. S. N. i. p. 533 (1788).

Querquedula carolinensis, Steph. Gen. Zool. xii. p. 148 ; Baird, B. of N. Amer. p. 777 ; Jard. Ann. & Mag. N. H. xx. (1817) p. 377 ('Tobago') ; Cab. J. f. Orn. 1857, p. 228 (Cuba) ; Moore, P. Z. S. 1859, p. 65 (Honduras) ; Scl. P. Z. S. 1857, p. 215, 1859, p. 370, 1860, p. 254 (Mexico) ; Scl. & Salv. Ibis. 1859, p. 231 (Honduras); Nomencl. p. 129.

Nettion carolinensis, March, Pr. Ac. Phil. 1861, p. 72 (Jamaica) ; Gundl. Repert. F.-N. i. p. 389, et J. für Orn. 1875, p. 381 (Cuba); Lawr. Mem. Bost. Soc. N. H. ii. p. 314 (Mexico).

Hab. Cuba (*Gundl.*) ; Jamaica (*March*) ; Tobago (*Kirk*) ; Mexico (*Sallé, De Oca, Grayson*) ; Honduras (*Dyson*).

The Green-winged Teal of the North-Americans occurs on passage in Cuba, but is rare. In Jamaica it is sometimes seen in autumn, but more generally in the spring. A single immature specimen was sent to Sir W. Jardine from Tobago by Mr. Kirk, who says that the species arrives in that island in October and November and departs in March or April. In Mexico it has been obtained at Mazatlan, Orizaba, and Jalapa. Leyland procured examples of it many years ago in Honduras, on the Aloor river. This is its furthest continental range to the south yet known to us.

4. QUERQUEDULA OXYPTERA.

Anas oxyptera, Meyen, Nov. Act. xvi. Suppl. p. 121, t. 26 (1833) (South Peru).

Querquedula oxyptera, Tsch. F. P. pp. 55, 309 (Sierra region of
Peru); Scl. & Salv. P. Z. S. 1867, p. 990 (S. Peru), 1868, p. 570,
1869, p. 157 (Peru); Nomencl. p. 129.
Querquedula angustirostris, Ph. & Landb. Wiegm. Arch. 1863,
pt. i. p. 202 (Tacna).

Supra pallide schistaceo-fusca, capite toto nigro frequenter trans-
fascioluto ; interscapulio rufescente lavato, plumis in centro
obscurioribus ; uropygio valde dilutiore ; speculo alari lato
nigro supra et subtus fascia ochracea terminato et fascia splen-
denti-æneo-viridi intus inclusa ; remigibus obscure schistaceis,
secundariorum marginibus utrinque pallide rufescentibus ; abdomine albo, pectore nigro punctato ; rostro flavo, culmine et
apice nigris ; pedibus corneis : long. tota 17·5, alæ 8·7, caudæ
4·0, tarsi 1·4, rostri a rictu 1·8.

Hab. Cordilleras of Peru, near Lake Titicaca (*Meyen*); Salinas
above Arequipa (*Whitely*) ; Laguna of Cucullata above Tacna (*Frobeen*).

This Duck was first discovered by Meyen, who obtained specimens of
it on the high cordillera of Peru, near Lake Titicaca. Meyen's name
(*oxyptera*) having been wrongly applied to the next species, Philippi
and Landbeck (as was pointed out by us in 1867) redescribed the
bird in 1863 under the name *angustirostris*. Their specimens were
obtained by Frobeen, on the Lake of Cucullata, in Southern Peru.

Our examples of this species were collected by Mr. Whitely on the
salt lake of Salinas, situated at an elevation of 14,000 feet above
Arequipa. Mr. Whitely subsequently procured other examples on
the lagoon of Tungasuca and on the river near Tinta, in the district
of Cuzco.

5. QUERQUEDULA FLAVIROSTRIS.

Pato pico amarillo y negro, Azara, Apunt. no. 439 (Buenos Ayres),
unde
Anas flavirostris, Vieill. N. D. v. p. 107 (1816), et Enc. Méth.
p. 353 (1823); Schl. Mus. des P.-B. *Anseres,* p. 59.
Querquedula flavirostris, Burm. J. f. Orn. 1860, p. 226, et La
Plata-Reise, ii. p. 516 (Mendoza); Scl. & Salv. P. Z. S. 1868,
p. 146 (Buenos Ayres), et Nomencl. p. 129.
Anas creccoides, King, Zool. Journ. iv. p. 99 (1828).
Querquedula creccoides, Eyton, Mon. Anat. p. 128 (1838); Gay,
Faun. Chil. p. 453 (1848); Cassin, Gilliss's Exp. ii. p. 203, t. xxvi.
(1856) (Chili); Darwin, Voy. Beagle, iii. p. 135 (1848); Scl.
P. Z. S. 1860, p. 389 (Falklands), 1867, p. 335 (Chili) ; Gould,
P. Z. S. 1859, p. 96 (Falklands); Ph. & Landb. Cat. Av. Chil.
p. 42 ; Abbott, Ibis, 1861, p. 160.
"*Querquedula oxyptera,* Meyen," Reich. Nat. t. lii. f. 164 ; Bibra,
Denkschr. Ak. Wien, v. p. 131 (1853) ; cf. J. f. Orn. 1855, p. 57
(Chili).

Similis præcedenti, sed minor, rostro breviore ; interscapulii plumis
in centro nigris, fuscescente ochraceo stricte marginatis ; uro-

pygio paululum obscuriore ; pectoris guttis magis distinctis et
fere totum ventrem occupantibus ; necnon alis et tarsis breviori-
bus distinguenda : long. tota 15·0, *alæ* 7·4, *caudæ* 3·5, *rostri a*
rictu 1·65, *tarsi* 1·2.

Hab. Buenos Ayres (*Azara, Hudson*): Mendoza (*Burm.*); Straits
of Magellan (*Darwin*): Falklands (*Abbott*) ; Chili (*Philippi &*
Landb).

This Duck was first obtained by Azara in Buenos Ayres : and his
name for it was not very correctly latinized by Vieillot. We have specimens from the same neighbourhood, obtained by Mr. W. H. Hudson.
It seems to be distributed thence all over Antarctic America. According to Burmeister it is not unfrequently seen near Mendoza, in the
lagoon of Rodeo del Medio. Philippi and Landbeck state that it is
common in Chili, and southwards on the western coast to the Straits
of Magellan. In the last-mentioned locality Mr. Darwin also obtained
specimens.

In the Falkland Islands this species is more plentiful in the interior than in the neighbourhood of civilization, and is found in large
flocks in some of the freshwater streams. It lays in September, and
even as early as August ; and the nest, with its complement of five
eggs, placed in the dry grass in some retired unfrequented valley,
is very difficult to find. As a rule, the bird is very tame.

6. QUERQUEDULA ANDIUM. (Plate XXXIV.)

Dafila ——, sp.?, Scl. P. Z. S. 1860, p. 83 (Ecuador).
Querquedula andium, Scl. & Salv. Nomencl. Av. Neotr. p. 162, et
P. Z. S. 1875, p. 237.

Capite undique nigro et albo frequentissime marmorato ; dorso
obscure cinereo, scapularibus æneo-nigris fusco circumcinctis ;
speculo alari æneo-nigro in secundariis dorso proximis nitidis-
sime æneo-viridi, supra et subtus fascia pallide castanea mar-
ginato ; abdomine albo cineraceo adumbrato ; pectore maculis
plumarum centralibus fusco-nigris ; rostro nigro, pedibus car-
neis : long. tota 16·0, *alæ* 9·0, *caudæ rigidiusculæ* 3·5.

Hab. High Ecuador, between Riobamba and Mocha (*Fraser*) ;
Sierra Nevada of Merida (*Goering*).

Obs. Similis Q. *oxypteræ* et Q. *flavirostri*, sed notæo obscuriore,
rostro nigro, et speculo alari æneo neque viridi distinguenda.

Mr. Fraser obtained a single specimen of this Duck on the high
plateau of Riobamba in 1859 ; but Sclater did not succeed in making
out the species. Subsequently Salvin selected two examples of the
same bird from a collection sent to this country from Quito ; and we
were thus enabled to describe it for the first time in our ' Nomenclator.'

Last year we had again the pleasure of recognizing an example of
this species in Mr. Goering's last collection from the Sierra Nevada
of Merida, where it was obtained at an altitude of 10,000 feet.

It would appear, therefore, that this Duck replaces the two preceding species in the Andes of Ecuador and Venezuela. We have
not yet seen it from Columbia ; but no doubt it occurs there also:

25*

7. QUERQUEDULA VERSICOLOR.

Pato pico de tres colores, Az. Apunt. no. 440 (Paraguay) undè
Anas versicolor, Vieill. N. D. v. p. 109 (1816), et Enc. Méth.
p. 353 (1823) ; Schl. Mus. des P. B. *Anseres*, p. 57.
Querquedula versicolor, Cassin in Gilliss's Exp. ii. p. 203 (1856)
(Chili) ; Scl. P. Z. S. 1860, p. 389 (Falklands) ; 1867, p. 335
(Chili) ; Abbott, Ibis, 1861, p. 161 (Falklands) ; Scl. & Salv.
P. Z. S. 1868, p. 146 (Buenos Ayres) ; Ibis, 1870, p. 499 (Sandy
Point), et Nomencl. p. 129 ; Salvin, Trans. Zool. Soc. iv. p. 499.
Anas maculirostris, Licht. Doubl. p. 81 (1823), ex Azara ; Burm.
J. für Orn. 1860, p. 266, et La Plata-Reise, ii. p. 516 (Mendoza) ;
Sund. P. Z. S. 1871, p. 126 (Galapagos).
Querquedula maculirostris, Gay, Faun. Chil. p. 452, Phil. &
Landb. Cat. Av. Chil. p. 42.
Pterocyanea maculirostris, Hartl. Ind. Az. p. 28.
Anas fretensis, King, P. Z. S. 1830-31, p. 15 ; Jard. & Selb. Ill.
Orn. iv. t. 29.
Cyanopterus fretensis, Eyton, Mon. Anat. p. 131 (1838).
Anas muralis, Merr. Ersch. & Grub. Enc. sect. i. vol. xxxv. p. 42.

*Supra nigra albo transfasciolata, fasciis in uropygio frequentiori-
bus et angustioribus ; pileo fumoso-nigro unicolori, capitis lateribus cum gutture lacteo-albis ; abdomine albido, in pectore
ochrascescente induto et nigro guttato, in vertice magis albicante
et nigro frequenter transfasciato ; alis extus grisescenti-fuscis ;
speculo purpurascenti-viridi, supra et subtus albo marginato et
subtus fascia altera subterminali nigra ornato ; hypochondriis
fasciis latis albis et nigris distincte notatis ; rostro nigro, macula
ad mandibulæ basin utrinque aurantiaca, pedibus corylinis : long.
tota 16·5, alæ 7·6, caudæ 3·4, tarsi 1·3, rostri a rictu 1·9.*
*Fem. mari similis sed coloribus paulo dilutioribus et speculo
alari obscuriore* [Descr. exempl. ex Chilia (*Leybold*)].

Hab. Paraguay (*Azara*) ; Buenos Ayres (*Hudson*) ; Mendoza
(*Burm.*) ; Magellan Straits (*King*) ; Falklands (*Abbott*) ; Chili
(*Phil. et Landb.*) ; Galapagos (*Sund.*).

This Duck, first described by Azara from Paraguay, is found all
over Antarctic America. Mr. Hudson obtained it at Conchitas near
Buenos Ayres ; and according to Burmeister it occurs at Mendoza
(at the foot of the Cordillera) near marshes and brooks.

In Chili Philippi and Landbeck found this species somewhat rarer
than Q. *cyanoptera*. In East Falkland it is not common ; but when it
does occur it is usually seen in numbers. It breeds in the Falklands ;
for Capt. Abbott had young birds brought to him, though he never
found a nest.

The supposed extension of the range of this Duck to the Galapagos is rather surprising. It rests upon the authority of Sundevall,
who determined the specimen.

8. QUERQUEDULA PUNA.

Anas puna, Tsch. Faun. Per. p. 309 (Peru) ; Burm. Syst. Ueb.
ii. p. 439.

Querquedula puna, Scl. & Salv. P. Z. S. 1869, p. 157 (Peru) ;
Ex. Orn. p. 197, t. 99, et Nomencl. p. 129.

*Supra pallide fuscescenti-cinerea, fusco variegata, plumis media-
liter obscurioribus ; pileo toto et linea nuchali nigris ; alis
extus fuscescenti-cinereis ; tectricibus minoribus plumbeo tinctis
et margine luto albo terminatis ; secundariis in pogonio externo
æneo-viridibus, albo late terminatis ; subtus ochraceo-alba, pectoris plumis fusco obsolete guttatis ; ventre toto et crisso nigricante minute transfasciolatis ; tectricibus subalaribus et plumis
axillaribus albis ; rostro (in ave viva) cæruleo, culmine nigricante ; pedibus cærulescenti-schistaceis : long. tota 18·0, alæ
8·5, caudæ 3, rostri a rictu 2·1, tarsi 1·3, dig. med. cum ungue
1·9.*

Hab. High Peru (*Philippi*); Bolivia, Cochabamba (*D'Orbigny*).

Obs. Affinis *Q. versicolori* sed rostro cærulescente, pileo nigro et
hypochondriorum fasciis angustis distinguenda.

The first examples of this fine Duck that attracted our notice were
those in the gallery of the Jardin des Plantes at Paris, one of which
is marked as having been obtained in the province of Cochabamba
in Bolivia by D'Orbigny, and the other in Chili by Mr. Gay, the
latter locality, however, being probably erroneous.

The specimens were not named ; and we were at first inclined to re-
gard them as belonging to an undescribed species. Subsequently, however, we received Peruvian skins of the same bird from Mr. H. Whitely,
and were thus induced to make a more accurate examination of it.
This led to the discovery that it is the species described by Tschudi
in his 'Fauna Peruana' as *Anas puna*, from a specimen obtained
by Philippi in the highlands of Peru, and transmitted to the Berlin
Museum. We should add that Sclater has examined the typical
example of *A. puna* in that collection, and is convinced of its identity
with the present bird.

Mr. Whitely obtained two examples of this Duck on the lagoon of
Tungasuca, which is situated in the Andes, south-east of Cusco, at an
elevation of about 12,000 feet above the sea-level. The skins are
both marked as "females ;" but the male, we suppose, would hardly
differ, except perhaps in possessing rather brighter plumage.

Mr. Whitely states that in the living bird the bill is light blue,
with a streak of black down the centre of the upper mandible, the
eye dark hazel, the legs and toes bluish slate-colour. He adds that
he met with this Duck in pairs, but found it rather rare.

Querquedula puna is a very well-marked species, and can hardly
be confounded with any other member of the family. It seems to be
most nearly allied to *Q. versicolor*, but is readily distinguishable by
its larger and uniformly coloured bill, blacker head, whiter throat,
and by the finer markings above and on the flanks.

9. QUERQUEDULA TORQUATA.

Pato collar negro, Azara, Apunt. no. 441 (Paraguay) undè
Anas torquata, Vieill. N. D. v. p. 110 (1816), et Enc. Méth.
p. 345 (1823) ; Schl. Mus. des P. B. *Anseres*, p. 61.

Querquedula torquata, Hartl. Ind. Az. p. 28 (1847) ; Gray, List
Gall. Grall. & Ans. B. M. p. 139 (1844) ; Scl. P. Z. S. 1867,
p. 335 (Chili) ; Scl. & Salv. P. Z. S. 1869, p. 635 (Buenos Ayres),
et Nomencl. Av. Neotr. p. 129.
Pato ceja blanca, Azara, Apunt, no. 442 (Paraguay), undè
Anas leucophrys, Vieill. N. D. v. p. 156 (1816), et Enc. Méth.
p. 354 (1823) ; Hartl. Ind. Az. p. 28 (♀).
A. rubidoptera, Dubois, Orn. Gal. p. 90, pl. lvii. (♂ et ♀) (1839).
A. rhodopus, Merrem, Ersch. & Grub. Enc. sect. i. vol. xxxv.
p. 42.

*Supra terreno-fusca, pileo et cervice in semitorquem posticum
utrinque expansis, tectricibus alarum minoribus, dorso postico
et cauda supra nigerrimis ; scapularibus pure castaneis ; alis
fusco-nigris, plaga magna in secundariorum tectricibus nivea,
secundariis ipsis extus viridi-œneis ; subtus capitis lateribus
cum gutture sordide albis fusco striolatis ; pectore rosaceo induto
et nigro sparse guttato ; ventre et hypochondriis albis griseo
tenuissime transfasciolatis, crisso medio nigro plaga utrinque
nivea ornato ; rostro nigro, pedibus flavissimis : long. tota 14·0,
alæ 7·2, caudæ 2·7, tarsi 1·1, rostri a rictu 1·7.   Fem. fusca,
superciliis et stria capitis utrinque cum gula et colli lateribus
albis ; subtus alba fusco transfasciata ; alis et cauda nigris ;
secundariis extus viridi-œneis ; alis macula magna alba, sicut
in mare, ornatis ; rostro rubro, pedibus flavis.*

Hab. Paraguay (*Azara*) ; Buenos Ayres (*Hudson*).
This fine Duck, for our first knowledge of which we are indebted
to Azara, is rather scarce in collections, and has yet only been recognized in few localities. Azara obtained examples of both the
somewhat dissimilar sexes in Paraguay, and described them under
different names, as was first pointed out by us (P. Z. S. 1869, p. 635)
from Mr. Hudson's specimens collected near Buenos Ayres. Philippi
and Landbeck (Cat. Av. Chil. p. 94) deny the occurrence of this
Duck in Chili, which Sclater had given on the authority of certain
specimens in the French national collection marked "Chili, Gay."
But we now know full well that Gay's localities are utterly untrust-
worthy.

10. QUERQUEDULA BRASILIENSIS.

Anas brasiliensis, Briss. Orn. iv. p. 360, undè
A. brasiliensis, Gm. S. N. i. p. 517 (1788) (Brazil) ; Max. Beitr.
v. p. 936 (Brazil) ; Cab. in Schomb. Guiana, iii. p. 762 (Guiana) ;
Burm. Syst. Ueb. iii. p. 437 ; J. für Orn. 1860, p. 267 ; La Plata-
Reise, ii. p. 517 (Tucuman) ; Schl. Mus. des P. B. *Anseres*, p. 61 ;
Reinh. Fugl. Bras. Camp. p. 21 (1870) (int. Brazil).
Querquedula brasiliensis, Scl. & Salv. P. Z. S. 1869, p. 635
(Buenos Ayres) ; Nomencl. p. 129 ; Pelz. Orn. Bras. p. 320 (1870).
"*Q. erythrorhyncha*, Spix," Eyton, Mon. Anat. p. 127 (1838) ;
Darwin, Voy. Beagle, iii. p. 135 (1841) (Buenos Ayres and Straits
of Magellan).
Ipicutiri, Az. Apunt. no. 437 (Paraguay), undè

Anas ipicutiri, Vieill. N. D. v. p. 120 (1816), et Enc. Méth. p. 351 (1823).

Querquedula ipicutiri, Hartl. Ind. Az. p. 28 (1847); Gay, Faun. Chil. p. 451 ; Ph. & Landb. Cat. Av. Chil. p. 42.

Anas paturi, Spix, Av. Bras. ii. p. 85, t. 109 (Rio S. Francisco).

A. notata, Licht. in Mus. Berol.

Supra fusca, pileo brunnescente; dorso postico, cauda et tectrici-bus alarum minoribus nigris: alis fusco-nigris, primariorum internorum et secundariorum pogoniis externis nitenti-æneo-viridibus, secundariorum internorum apicibus latis niveis, a colore æneo fascia nigra disjunctis ; subtus dilutior, in pectore rubiginoso lavata, gutture albidiore, ventris plumis fusco obsolete transfasciatis; rostro nigricante, pedibus flavis: long. tota 15·5, alæ 7, caudæ 3·3, tarsi 1·2, rostri a rictu 1·8.

Hab. Guiana (*Schomb.*) ; Rio Brancho (*Natt.*) ; Rio San Francisco (*Spix*) ; S. E. Brazil (*Max. et Burm.*) ; S. Paulo and Mato-grosso (*Natt.*) ; Bolivia (*Pearce*) ; Paraguay (*Azara*) ; Buenos Ayres (*Hudson*) ; Paraná and Tucuman (*Burm.*) ; Magellan Straits (*Darwin*).

This Duck seems to be very widely extended in Eastern South America from the north down to the extreme south. Schomburgk found it abundant in the marshy savannas of British Guiana ; and Natterer obtained specimens on the Rio Brancho. In S.E. Brazil it is said by Prince Maximilian to be the commonest species of Duck. According to Azara, *Q. brasiliensis* is much more abundant in Para-guay than in Buenos Ayres. It is usually seen in pairs, but some-times in flocks of twenty, associating with other Ducks. He adds that it moults in May and nests in August.

Burmeister says this species is very common on the Paraná and in all marshes and lagoons of the northern districts. It is also common at Tucuman. Mr. Darwin obtained specimens from Buenos Ayres in October, and from the Straits of Magellan in February.

Gay has inserted this species (like many others) in his list of Chilian birds; but Philippi and Landbeck (Cat. Av. Chil. p. 42) state that so far as they know it does not occur in that Republic. Gay's specimen was probably from Bolivia, whence Salvin has obtained an example.

Genus 7. DAFILA.   Type.

Dafila, Stephens, G. Z. xii. pt. 2, p. 126 (1824).. *D. acuta.*

Phasianurus, Wagler, Isis, 1832, p. 1235 ......*D. acuta.*

Pœcilonetta, Eyton, Mon. Anat. p. 32 (1838).... *D. bahamensis.*

Three Pintails are met with in the Neotropical Region. One of these is the well-known European bird which penetrates in winter into the northern portion of the region ; the others are endemic southern species, one of which is sometimes separated as generically distinct.

1. DAFILA ACUTA.

Anas acuta, Linn. S. N. i. p. 202 (1766).

Dafila acuta, Baird, B. of N. Am. p. 776 ; Cab. J. für Orn. 1857,

p. 227 (Cuba) ; Scl. P. Z. S. 1857, p. 206 (Jalapa, Mexico); Scl.
et Salv. Ibis, 1859, p. 231 (Guatemala), et Nomencl. Av. Neotr.
p. 130 ; March, Pr. Ac. Phil. 1864, p. 71 (Jamaica); Lawr. Ann.
Lyc. N. Y. viii. p. 13 (Panama), et ix. (1868) p. 143 (Costa Rica) ;
Mem. Bost. Soc. N. H. ii. p. 314 (Mexico); Gundl. Repert. F.-N.
i. p. 388, et J. für Orn. 1875, p. 378 (Cuba).

Hab. Cuba (*Gundlach*) ; Jamaica (*March*) ; Mexico, Jalapa
(*Sallé*); Mazatlan (*Grayson*); Coahuaha (*Xantus*); Belize (*Salvin*);
Guatemala, Dueñas (*Salvin*) ; Costa Rica (*Lawrence*) ; Panama
(*M'Leannan*).

In Cuba the Pintail is very common on passage during the winter
and autumnal months. It also occurs in Jamaica in numbers as a
winter visitant. It was seen at Belize by Salvin, and is a common
visitor to the Lake of Dueñas in winter. Its furthest recorded locality south appears to be the isthmus of Panama, where M'Leannan
found it.

2. DAFILA SPINICAUDA.

Pato cola aguda, Az. Apunt. no. 429 (Buenos Ayres), undè
Anas spinicauda, Vieill. N. D. v. p. 135 (1816) et Enc. Méth.
p. 356; Burm. La Plata-Reise, ii. p. 515 ; Schl. Mus. de P.-B.
Anseres, p. 39.
Erismatura spinicauda, Hartl. Ind. Az. p. 27 ; Pelz. Orn. Bras.
p. 321 (1870).
Dafila spinicauda, Scl. P. Z. S. 1870, p. 665, t. xxxviii. (Chili) ;
Scl. & Salv. P. Z. S. 1868, p. 146 (Rep. Arg.), 1869, p. 157 (Tinta,
Peru), et Nomencl. Av. Neotr. p. 130.
Anas oxyura, Meyen, Nov. Act. xiv. Suppl. p. 122 (1833) ;
Merrem, Ersch. & Gruber's Enc. sect. i. vol. xxxv. p. 43 ; Gay, Faun.
Chil. p. 449 (1848); Cassin, Gilliss's Exp. ii. p. 202 (1856); Burm. La
Plata-Reise, ii. p. 515 (Mendoza) ; Scl. P. Z. S. 1867, p. 335 (Chili) ;
Ph. & Landb. Cat. Av. Chil. p. 41.
Dafila urophasianus, Scl. P. Z. S. 1860, p. 389 (Falklands) ;
Abbott, Ibis, 1861, p. 160 (Falklands).
Dafila —— sp.? Scl. & Salv. Ibis, 1868, p. 189 (Sandy Point).
Anas caudacuta, Burm. J. für Orn. 1860, p. 266 (Mendoza).

*Supra fusca, plumis in centro nigricantibus fusco circumdatis ;
pileo læte rufescente nigro punctulato ; alis extus fuscis, speculo alari amplo æneo-nigro, fascia lata cerrina utrinque marginato ; subtus pectore et hypochondriis cum crisso rufescentibus,
plumis in centro nigris ; gutture sordide albo parce nigro punctato ; ventre albo in parte inferiore fusco obsolete variegato ;
rostro nigro, mandibula ad basin utrinque flava ; pedibus plumbeis : long. tota 19·0, alæ 9·7, caudæ rectr. med. 5·5, ext. 3,
rostri a rictu 2·3, tarsi 1·6.* Fem. mari similis.
Hab. S. Brazil, S. Paulo (*Natt.*) ; Monte Video (*Sellow*); Buenos
Ayres (*Azara, Hudson*); Rio Paraná et Mendoza (*Burm.*); Magellan Straits (*Cunningh.*); Falklands (*Abbott*); Chili (*Phil. et
Landb.*); S. Peru, Tinta (*Whitely*).

This Pintail has a wide distribution in Antarctic America, extend-

ing from S. Brazil on one coast and the highlands of Peru on the
western side down to the Magellan Straits and the Falklands.
Azara, its original discoverer, gives no particulars respecting its
history, merely saying that he obtained four similar specimens in
Buenos Ayres. It was procured in the adjoining State of Monte
Video by Sellow, and in the Brazilian province of São Paulo by
Natterer. Burmeister says this Duck is not unfrequently found in the
lagoons bordering the Paraná. In his ' La Plata-Reise ' he distinguishes a western race from the vicinity of Mendoza, for which he
adopts Meyen's term *oxyura*. But after comparing eastern and
western specimens together, we are of opinion that they belong to
one species.

In Chili Philippi and Landbeck say that this is the commonest
species of Duck. In the Falkland Islands it occurs rather sparingly
in the freshwater ponds of the interior, where it resides throughout
the year. The species is also found on the adjoining coast of Patagonia ; and the specimen in Dr. Cunningham's collection left unde-
termined in our first list of his birds (' Ibis,' 1868, p. 189) certainly
belongs to it, though not in full plumage. Mr. Whitely has sent
several skins of this Duck home from the Cuzcan Andes, obtained
on the lake of Tungasuca and on the river near Tinta.

3. DAFILA BAHAMENSIS.

Ilathera Duck (*Anas bahamensis*), Catesby, Carolina, vol. i.
p. 93, t. 93, undè

Anas bahamensis, Linn. S. N. i. p. 199 (1766) ; Max. Beitr. iv.
p. 925 (S.E. Brazil) ; Burm. Syst. Ueb. iii. p. 436 ; J. für Orn.
1860, p. 266, et La Plata-Reise, ii. p. 515 (Uruguay) ; Schl. Mus.
des P.-B. *Anseres*, p. 55.

Dafila bahamensis, Hartl. Ind. Az. p. 27 (1847) ; Cab. in Schom-
burgk's Guiana, iii. p. 763 ; Gay, Faun. Chil. vol. i. p. 448 (1848) ;
Cassin, Gilliss's Exp. ii. p. 203 (1856) ; Scl. P. Z. S. 1867, p. 335
(Chili) ; Ph. & Landb. Cat. Av. Chil. p. 41 ; Scl. & Salv. P. Z. S.
1868, p. 146 (Rep. Arg.), 1870, p. 323 (Galapagos), et Nom. Av.
Neotr. p. 130 ; Pelz. Orn. Bras. p. 320 (1870) ; Salvin, Trans. Zool.
Soc. iv. p. 499.

Pœcilonetta bahamensis, Eyton, Mon. Anat. p. 116 (1838) ;
Sclater, P. Z. S. 1860, p. 389 (Falklands) ; Darwin, Voy. Beagle, iii.
p. 135 (Galapagos Islands) ; Abbott, Ibis, 1861, p. 160 (Falklands).

Anas fimbriata, Merrem, Ersch. u. Grub. Enc. sect. i. vol. xxxv.
p. 35 (ex Azara).

Anas urophasianus, Vig. Zool. Journ. iv. p. 357 (1829) ; Zool.
Beechey's Voy. p. 31, t. 14.

Dafila urophasianus, Eyton, Mon. Anat. p. 112, t. 20 (1838).

Anas ilathera, Vieill. Enc. Méth. p. 152 (1823), ex Brisson,
Orn. iv. p. 360.

Pato pico aplomado y roxo, Az. Apunt. no. 433 (Buenos Ayres),
undè

Anas rubrirostris, Vieill. N. D. v. p. 108 (1816), et Enc. Méth.
p. 353 (1823).

Rufescenti-fusca, plumis in centro nigricantibus; dorso postico nigricante; tectricibus caudæ superioribus cum cauda cervinis, rectricibus mediis dilutioribus; alis obscure schistaceo-nigris, speculo læte æneoviridi, supra et subtus fascia saturate cervina marginato et fascia altera subterminali subtus ornato; secundariorum intimorum marginibus externis cervinis, cum speculi marginibus concoloribus; subtus fuscescenti-cervina, omnino obsolete nigro guttata, gutture toto cum genis et cervice antica pure albis; rostro nigro, macula ad basin utrinque rubra; pedibus fuscis: long. tota 18·0, *alæ* 8·4, *caudæ rectr. med.* 5, *ext.* 2·8, *tarsi* 1·5, *rostri a rictu* 1·9. Fem. *mari similis.*

Hab. British Guiana *(Schomb.)* ; Praia de Cajutuba, near Para *(Natt.)* ; S.E. Brazil *(Max. et Burm.)* ; Buenos Ayres *(Azara et Burm.)* ; Patagonia *(Darwin, King)* ; Falklands *(Abbott)* ; Chili *(Ph. et Landb.)* ; Galapagos *(Darwin et Habel).*

Linnæus established his *Anas bahamensis* upon the Ilathera Duck of Catesby, of which that author tells us a single specimen was procured in the Bahama Islands. Catesby's figure most undoubtedly represents the present species ; but if his locality is correct, the bird obtained was probably a straggler, as we have no other authentic record of its occurrence north of Guiana, where Schomburgk noticed it in flocks on the mouths of the rivers. Azara obtained two specimens of this Duck in a lagoon on the pampas of Buenos Ayres ; and Darwin records it from Bahia Blanca in Northern Patagonia. Burmeister says it is spread abundantly over the whole of Brazil in ponds and marshes, and that it is nearly the commonest species of Duck there. He also observed it numerous in the La-Plata district, as well as on the Rio Uruguay. It is also common near Buenos Ayres, and is often seen exposed for sale in the market. On the Paraná and further westwards Burmeister did not observe it.

In Chili it is of uncertain occurrence, some years there being none to be seen, whilst in others it appears in plenty. Philippi and Landbeck remark that it is also found in Peru ; but we have not yet seen examples from that locality. Mr. Darwin procured one specimen from a small salt-water lagoon in the Galapagos archipelago in the month of October ; and Dr. Habel also obtained three individuals in that group of islands, and says it is not uncommon there. In the Falkland Islands it appears as a straggler from the mainland.

Genus 8. MARECA.   Type.

Mareca, Stephens, G. Z. xii. pt. 2, p. 130 (1824). . *M. penelope.*

Two Widgeons occur within the limits of the Neotropical Region, one of which is a winter migrant from the north, the other a peculiar Antarctic species of rather abnormal form.

1. MARECA AMERICANA.

Le Canard jensen, Buff. Pl. Enl. 955, undè

Anas americana, Gm. S. N. p 526 (1788).

Mareca americana, Steph. G. Z. xii. pt. 2, p. 135 ; Baird, B. of N. Am. p. 783 ; Cab. J. für Orn. 1857, p. 227 (Cuba) ; Scl. &

Salv. Ibis, 1859, p. 231 (Guatemala), Nomencl. Av. Neotr. p. 130 ;
Newton, Ibis, 1860, p. 308 (St. Thomas); Salv. Ibis, 1865, p. 193;
March, Pr. Ac. Phil. 1864, p. 71 (Jamaica) ; Léot. Ois. Trin. p. 511
(Trinidad); Gundl. Repert. F.-N. i. p. 388, et J. für Orn. 1875,
p. 378 (Cuba); Lawr. Mem. Bost. Soc. N. H. ii. p. 315 (Mexico).
    Hab. Mexico (*Grayson*); Guatemala (*Salvin*); Cuba (*Gundl.*) ;
Jamaica (*March*); St. Thomas (*Newton*) ; Trinidad (*Léotaud*).
    The American Widgeon is said to be very common in Cuba during
the annual migration from September to April. In Jamaica, too, it
is to be seen in all its forms and variety of plumage.   Mr. Riise
procured specimens in St. Thomas; and Léotaud records it as a
regular winter visitant to Trinidad.   In Central America it likewise
occurs in winter, having been found by Salvin in all the Guatemalan
lakes during that season.

2. MARECA SIBILATRIX.

Anas sibilatrix, Poeppig, Fror. Not. no. 529 (1829), p. 10
(Chili).
Anas chiloensis, King, P. Z. S. 1830–31, p. 15 ; Burm. J. für Orn.
1860, p. 227, et La Plata-Reise, ii. p. 517 (Mendoza) ; Schl. Mus.
P.-B. *Anseres*, p. 46.
Mareca chiloensis, Eyton, Mon. Anat. p. 117, t. xxi. (1838);
Hartl. Ind. Az. p. 27 (1847) ; Gay, Faun. Chil. p. 447 (1848);
Cassin, Gilliss's Exp. ii. p. 201 (1856); Gould, P. Z. S. 1859, p. 96
(Falklands) ; Phil. & Landb. Cat. Av. Chil. p. 41 ; Scl. P. Z. S.
1860, p. 389 (Falklands); 1867, pp. 335 (Chili); 1870, p. 665
Chili ; Scl. & Salv. P. Z. S. 1869, p. 635 (Rep. Arg.); Ibis, 1869
p. 284 (Gregory Bay), et Nomencl. Av. Neotr. p. 130.
Pato pico pequeno, Az. Apunt. no. 432 (Buenos Ayres).
Anas parvirostris, Merr. Ersch. u. Grub. Enc. sect. i. vol. xxxv.
p. 43 (1841).

  *Supra nigra, in cervice albo transfasciata, dorsi et scapularium
  plumis albo utrinque marginatis ; pileo et genis pure albis, nucha
  et cervice postica viridi-purpureo lucentibus ; alis fuscis, tectricibus minoribus albis; secundariis velutino-nigris ad basin albis;
  subtus alba, gutture et cervice antica nigricantibus, pectore superiore nigro albo transfasciolato, hypochondriis ferrugineolavatis;
  rostro et pedibus nigris: long. tota 20·0, alæ 10·3, caudæ 4·3,
  tarsi 1·4, rostri a rictu 1·6.   Fem. mari similis sed paulo
  obscurior.*

  Hab. Paraguay (*Azara*); Buenos Ayres and Mendoza (*Burm.*) ;
Falklands (*Abbott*); Chiloe (*King*) ; Valdivia and Central Chili
(*Phil. et Landb.*).
    Azara was the original describer of this fine Duck, from specimens
obtained in Buenos Ayres ; but Vieillot appears to have missed
giving any Latin appellation to the species ; and it was first provided
with a scientific name by Poeppig, who gave an excellent description
of it in his "Fragmenta Zoologica Itineris Chilensis," published in
Froriep's 'Notizen' for July 1829. This was two years before
Capt. King's term *chiloensis* (usually employed for this species) ap-

peared; and we have consequently found it necessary to revert to the older name.

This Duck is found near Mendoza, according to Burmeister, at the foot of the Cordilleras in the lagoons and rivers. It also occurs in the lakes of the Pampas and near Buenos Ayres, where birds are often sold in the market. In Southern Chili and Valdivia, as stated by Philippi and Landbeck, it is a rare species, but is more common in the central provinces. It is one of the wildest and scarcest birds in East Falkland. Capt. Abbott never found its nest, but says that young ones were seen in a pond near Port Louis in January.

Genus 9. SPATULA.   Type.

Spatula, Boié, Isis, 1822, p. 563. . . . . *S. clypeata.*
Rhynchaspis, Stephens, G. Z. xii. pt. 2, p. 114 (1824). *S. clypeata.*

Two Shovellers are likewise found within Neotropical boundaries. One of them is a northern immigrant, only met with in the Antilles ; the other a fine well-marked southern endemic species.

1. SPATULA CLYPEATA.

Anas clypeata, Linn. S. N. i. p. 200 (1766).
Spatula clypeata, Boie, Isis, 1822, p. 564; Baird, B. N. Am. p. 781; Scl. & Salv. Ibis, 1859, p. 231 (Guatemala), et Nom. Av. Neotr. p. 130; Scl. P. Z. S. 1862, p. 20 (Mexico); Newton, Ibis, 1860, p. 308 (St. Thomas) ; March, Pr. Ac. Phil. 1864, p. 71 (Jamaica) ; Gundl. Repert. F.-N. i. p. 389, et J. für Orn. 1875, p. 379 (Cuba) ; Léot. Ois. Trin. p. 518 (1866) (Trinidad); Lawr. Mem. Bost. Soc. N. II. ii. p. 314 (Mexico).
Rhynchaspis clypeata, Cab. J. für Orn. 1857, p. 228 (Cuba).

Hab. Mexico (*Boucard, Grayson*) ; Guatemala (*Salvin*) ; Cuba (*Gundlach*) ; Jamaica (*March*).

In Cuba, according to Dr. Gundlach, the Shoveller is a regular winter visitant, remaining from September to April. It also appears in Jamaica in considerable numbers. In Mexico it has been found at Guaymas and Mazatlan, as well as in S. Mexico. In Guatemala it is common in winter.

2. SPATULA PLATALEA.

Pato espatulato, Az. Apunt. no. 431 (Buenos Ayres), undè
Anas platalea, Vieill. N. D. v. p. 157 (1816), et Enc. Méth. p. 357 (1823) ; Burm. La Plata-Reise, ii. p. 517 (Panama and Buenos Ayres) ; Schl. Mus. des P.-B. *Anseres*, p. 35.
Spatula platalea, Hartl. Ind. Az. p. 27 ; Scl. P. Z. S. 1867, p. 335 (Chili) ; Scl. & Salv. P. Z. S. 1868, p. 145 (Buenos Ayres), et Nomencl. Av. Neotr. p. 130.
Rhynchaspis maculatus, Gould, MS.; Jard. & Selb. Ill. Orn. t. 147; Eyton, Mon. Anat. p. 134 (1838); Phil. & Landb. Cat. Av. Chil. p. 43.
Dafila cæsio-scapulata, Reich. Natat. tab. li. f. 180 ; Bibra,

Denkschr. Ak. Wien, v. p. 131 (1853), et J. für Orn. 1855, p. 57 (Chili).

Rhynchaspis mexicana, Licht. Nomencl. p. 102 (descr. nulla) (?).

Supra et subtus rufescens, nigro guttata, capite et cervice undique dilutioribus et maculis minutis aspersis; uropygio nigro; dorso postico nigricante rufo undulato ; alis fusco-nigris, tectricibus minoribus cæruleis, intermediis albis ; secundariis extus æneis viridi nitentibus, scapularibus et secundariis dorsi proximis linea scapum occupante alba ornatis ; crisso nigro; cauda fusca, rectricibus lateralibus extus albo marginatis ; rostro (in pelle) obscuro; pedibus flavis : long. tota 20·5, alæ 8·0, caudæ 4·5, tarsi 1·4, rostri a rictu 2·7.   Fem. supra nigricanti-fusca, plumarum marginibus cervino-rufis; tectricibus alarum minoribus cærulescente lavatis ; subtus cervino-rufescens nigro variegata et obsolete punctata ; gula fere immaculata, crassitie minore.

Hab. Buenos Ayres (*Azara & Hudson*); Paraná (*Burm.*); Chili (*Phil. & Landb.*); Falklands (*Leconte*).

According to Azara this species of Shoveller is found both in Paraguay and in Buenos Ayres. Burmeister also met with it on the Paraná and near Buenos Ayres. In Chili Philippi and Landbeck state that it is common in the central provinces, but rarer towards the south. Mr. Darwin obtaind his specimen of this Shoveller from the Rio de La Plata ; whence also the one described in Jardine and Selby's 'Illustrations of Ornithology,' under the name of *Rhynchaspis maculatus,* was procured by Mr. Gould.

A female of this species, in Salvin and Godman's collection, was obtained in the Falklands by Leconte when he went to obtain living Sea-lions in 1867.

Genus 10. Aix.

		Type.
Aix, Boié, Isis, 1828, p. 329	....	*A. sponsa.*
Dendronessa, Sw Faun. Bor.-Am. Birds, p. 497 (1831).		*A. sponsa.*
Lampronessa, Wagler, Isis, 1832, p. 282	....	*A. sponsa.*

Aix is an Arctic form, the American species of which has diffused itself as far south as Cuba and Jamaica.

AIX SPONSA.

Anas sponsa, Linn. S. N. i. p. 207 (1766).

Aix sponsa, Boié, Isis, 1828, p. 329 ; Baird, B. of N. Am. p. 785 ; Gundl. J. für Orn. 1857, p. 226, Repert. F.-N. i. p. 389, et J. für Orn. 1875, p. 381 (Cuba); March, Pr. Ac. Phil. 1864, p. 71 (Jamaica); Scl. & Salv. Nom. Av. Neotr. p. 130; Lawr. Mem. Bost. Soc. ii. p. 315 (Mexico).

Hab. Mexico (*Abert*) ; Cuba (*Gundl.*); Jamaica (*March*).

A resident species in Cuba, frequenting shady lagoons. It nests in the island ; but at what time of year Dr. Gundlach had not ascertained. In Jamaica it is very rare. Mr. Lawrence gives Col. Abert as the authority for its occurrence near Mazatlan, Mexico.

Subfamily IV. FULIGULINÆ.

The Sea-ducks are essentially arctic in their distribution. One peculiar form only (*Micropterus*) occurs on the coast of Antarctic America. A second form (*Metopiana*), though belonging to this group, seems to be only met with on fresh water.

Genus 1. METOPIANA.

Type.

Metopiana, Bp. C. R. xliii. p. 146 (1856) ...... *M. peposaca.*

Some authors have been inclined to associate this peculiar Duck with the Anatinæ; but though it is, we believe, strictly an inhabitant of fresh water, and has not the lobated hind toe of the typical Fuligulinæ, it possesses their peculiarity in the structure of the trachea, as mentioned by Burmeister (La-Plata Reise, ii. p. 518), and as recently described and figured by Garrod (P. Z. S. 1875, p. 154).

METOPIANA PEPOSACA.

Pato negrizco ala blanca, Az. Apunt. no. 430 (Paraguay and Buenos Ayres), undè

Anas peposaca, Vieill. N. D. v. p. 132 (1816), et Enc. Méth. p. 357 (1823); Hartl. Ind. Az. p. 27; Burm. La Plata-Reise, ii. p. 518, J. für Orn. 1860, p. 227 (Paraná).

Fuligula peposaca, Schl. Mus. des P.-B. *Anseres*, p. 31.

Anas metopias, Pöppig, Fror. Notiz. no. 529, p. 9 (1829).

Fuligula metopias, Gay, Faun. Chil. p. 456 (1848); Hartl. Naum. 1853, p. 217; Cassin, Gilliss's Exp. ii. p. 204, t. xxvii. (1856) Chili; Scl. P. Z. S. (1867), 335; Reich. Nat. t. cclxxxv. f. 2350; Phil. & Landb. Cat. Av. Chil. p. 43.

Metopiana peposaca, Bp. C. R. xliii. p. 146 (1856); Scl. & Salv. P. Z. S. 1868, p. 146 (Buenos Ayres), et Nom. Av. Neotr. p. 130; Scl. P. Z. S. 1870, p. 666, t. 37; Garrod, P. Z. S. 1875, p. 154.

Anas albipennis, Licht. MS.

Nigra, in dorso minutissime albo irrorata, cervice postica et capite superiore toto nitore purpureo indutis; secundariis albis, nigro terminatis et tectricibus nigris obtectis, speculum album efficientibus; primariis grisescenti-albis, horum quatuor externis in pogonio exteriore et omnium apicibus nigris; ventre toto griseo et albo minutissime vermiculato; crisso albo; rostro rosaceo, ad basin tumido; pedibus flavis: long. tota 19·0, alæ 9·4, caudæ 2·8, tarsi 1·7, rostri a rictu 2·3. Fem. supra brunnea, campterio et speculo alari albis; subtus alba, pectore et hypochondriis rufescenti-brunneis, rostro obscuro, pedibus corneis (Descr. exempl. ex Monte Video).

Hab. Paraguay (*Azara*); Buenos Ayres (*Hudson*); Monte Video Johnston in *Mus. S.-G.*); Paraná (*Burm.*); Chili (*Phil. et Landb.*).

This beautiful Duck was first obtained by Azara, who, however, gives no details respecting it; but Burmeister tells us it is very common on the Parana; and Mr. Hudson obtained specimens near Buenos Ayres. In the central part of Chili, Philippi and Landbeck state that it is common, but rare in the southern provinces.

Judging from the description of Prince Maximilian, his *Anas erythrophthalma* (Beitr. iv. p. 929), as already suggested by Salvin (Ibis, 1874, p. 319), would appear to be very closely allied to the present species, if not identical with it. The male, as described, seems to be in immature plumage. The female agrees tolerably well with that of the present bird. Prince Maximilian obtained his two specimens of *A. erythrophthalma* in a small lake near Villa de Belmonte, in S.E. Brazil, in the month of November. No subsequent travellers seem to have recognized the species so far north.

The Rosy-billed Duck has been successfully introduced into Europe, and has bred on more than one occasion in our Gardens. In the 'Proceedings' for 1870 (*l. s. c.*) Sclater has given an account of it, and figures of both sexes from the living birds.

Genus 2. FULIGULA.　　Type.

Branta, Boié, Isis, 1822, p. 561 (nec Scop.).. **F. rufina.**
Fuligula, Stephens, G. Z. xii. pt. 2, p 187 .. **F. rufina.**
Callichen, Brehm, Vög. Deutschl. p. 921 (1831) **F. rufina.**
Fulix, Sund. Vet. Ak. Handl. 1835, p. 129 (1836) **=*Fuligula*.**
Nyroca, Fleming *, Phil. of Zool. ii. p. 260 (1822) **F. leucophthalma.**
Aythya, Boié, Isis, 1822, p. 564............ **F. ferina.**
Marila, Reichenb. Nat. Syst. p. ix. (1852) .. **F. ferina.**

Fuligula, as here considered, is a purely northern form, of which five species occur in winter within the Neotropical Region.

1. FULIGULA MARILA.

Anas marila, Linn. S. N. i. p. 196.
Fuligula marila, Stephens, Zool. xii. p. 198.
Fulix marila, Baird, B. N. A. p. 791 ; Lawrence, Mem. Bost. Soc. N. H. ii. p. 315 (Mazatlan).

Hab. Mazatlan, Mexico (*Grayson*).
Col. Grayson found the Scaup near Mazatlan in the winter months.

2. FULIGULA AFFINIS.

Fuligula affinis, Eyton, Mon. Anat. p. 157 (1838) ; Gosse, B. Jamaica, p. 408 ; Scl. & Salv. Ibis, 1859, p. 231 (Guatemala) Salv. P. Z. S. 1870, p. 219 (Veragua).
Fulix affinis, Baird, B. of N. Am. p. 791 ; Gundl. Repert. F.-N. i. p. 390, et J. für Orn. 1875, p. 382 (Cuba); Lawr. Ann. Lyc. N. Y. ix. (1868), p. 143 (Costa Rica); March, Pr. Ac. Phil. 1864, p. 71 (Jamaica); A. & E. Newton, Ibis, 1859, p. 366 (St. Croix); Scl. et Salv. Nom. Av. Neotr. p. 130 ; Lawr. Ann. Lyc. N. Y. ix. p. 210 (Yucatan), et Mem. Bost. Soc. N. H. ii. p. 315 (Mexico).
Fuligula mariloides, Cab. J. für Orn. 1857, p. 230 (Cuba).
Fuligula marila, Jard. Ann. & Mag. N. H. xx. 1847, p. 377 (To-bago); Léot. Ois. Trin. p. 522 (1866) (Trinidad).

Hab. Cuba (*Gundlach*); Jamaica (*March*); Tobago (*Kirk*);

---

* Fleming puts *Anas ferina* first on the list: but *A. nyroca* should be considered his type, if that bird is separated from *Fuligula*.

Trinidad (*Léotaud*); Mexico (*Grayson*); Yucatan (*Schott*); Guatemala (*Salvin*); Costa Rica (*c. Frantzius*); Veragua (*Arcé*).

This Duck is rather rare in Cuba, but occurs during the autumnal and winter months on passage on the large lagoons which are not choked with high reeds. In Jamaica it is seen in considerable numbers in winter. Mr. Kirk also records it from Tobago, but says it is very rare; and Léotaud gives it as a frequent visitor to Trinidad, where it arrives in November, and departs in April.

In Guatemala Salvin found it abundant on the lakes in winter; v. Frantzius obtained it in Costa Rica; and Arcé has sent specimens from Veragua.

3. FULIGULA COLLARIS.

Anas collaris, Donov. Brit. B. vi. t. 147 (1809).
Fuligula rufitorques, Gosse, B. Jamaica, p. 408; Sclater, P. Z. S. 1862, p. 20.
Fuligula collaris, Cab. J. für Orn. 1857, p. 230 (Cuba); Salv. & Scl. Ibis, 1860, p. 277 (Guatemala).
Fuligula affinis, Scl. P. Z. S. 1859, p. 369 (err.).
Fulix collaris, Baird, B. of N. Am. p. 792; March, Pr. Ac. Phil. 1864, p. 72 (Jamaica); Gundl. Repert. F.-N. i. p. 390, et J. für Orn. 1875, p. 383 (Cuba); Lawr. Mem. Bost. Soc. N. II. ii. p. 315 (Mazatlan); Scl. et Salv. Nom. Av. Neotr. p. 130.

Hab. Cuba (*Gundlach*); Jamaica (*March*); E. Mexico (*Boucard*); N.W. Mexico (*Grayson et Xantus*); Guatemala (*Salvin*).

One of the commonest of the northern migrants in Cuba, where it frequents open lagoons not choked with reeds. In Jamaica it is rarely met with.

We have examined Mexican skins of this Duck collected by Boucard and De Oca; and Salvin found it on the lakes of Guatemala sparingly in winter.

4. FULIGULA AMERICANA.

Fuligula americana, Eyton, Mon. Anat. p. 155 (1838).
Aythya americana, Baird, B. of N. Am. p. 793; Gosse, B. Jamaica, p. 408, et March, Pr. Ac. Phil. 1864, p. 72 (Jamaica); Scl. et Salv. Nom. Av. Neotr. p. 130; Lawr. Mem. Bost. Soc. N. II. ii. p. 315 (Mexico).

Hab. Jamaica (*March*); valley of Mexico (*Le Strange*); Mazatlan (*Grayson*).

According to Mr. March this Pochard is not uncommon in Jamaica in winter. We know of but few instances of its occurrence on the mainland within the limits of the Neotropical region. Mr. Le Strange brought one specimen from the valley of Mexico; and Col. Grayson obtained it at Mazatlan.

5. FULIGULA VALISNERIA.

Anas valisneria, Wills. Am. Orn. viii. p. 103, t. 70 (1814).
Fuligula valisneria, Cab. J. für Orn. 1857, p. 230 (Cuba).

Aythya valisneria, Baird, B. of N. Am. p. 794; March, Pr. Ac. Phil. 1864, p. 72 (Jamaica) ; Salv. Ibis, 1866, p. 198 (Guatemala) ; Gundl. Repert. F.-N. i. p. 390, et J. für Orn. 1875, p. 382 (Cuba) ; Scl. et Salv. Nom. Av. Neotr. p. 130 ; Lawr. Mem. Bost. Soc. N. II. ii. p. 315 (Mexico).

Hab. Cuba (*Gundlach*) ; Jamaica (*March*) ; Mexico (*Grayson*); Guatemala (*Salvin*).

An occasional winter visitant in Cuba, having been observed by Dr. Gundlach in some numbers in 1839 and 1850. Mr. March says that it is sometimes found in Jamaica in company with the Pintail. Col. Grayson found it at Mazatlan.

Salvin once killed a single specimen of the Canvas-back on the Lake of Dueñas ; but this is the only instance of its occurrence so far south that we are acquainted with.

Genus 3. CLANGULA.   Type.

Clangula, Fleming, Phil. of Zool. ii. p 260 (1822) *C. glaucion**. *Glaucion*, Kaup, Nat. Syst. p. 53 (1829) . . . . *C. glaucion*. *Bucephala*, Baird, B. of N. A. p. 796 (1860) . . . *C. albeola*.

Clangula is another high northern genus, of which two species have been casually met with just within the confines of the Neotropical Region.

1. CLANGULA GLAUCION.

Anas clangula et *A. glaucion*, Linn. S. N. i. p. 201.¯ *Clangula americana*, Cab. J. für Orn. 1857, p. 230 (Cuba). *Bucephala americana*, Baird, B. of N. Am. p. 796; Lawr. Mem. Bost. Soc. N. II. ii. p. 315 (Mexico).

Hab. Cuba (*Lembeye*) ; Mexico (*Grayson*).

Dr. Gundlach tells us that Lembeye *believed* he had seen an example of the Golden-eye on a pool in Cuba, but was not able to get it. We observe that Dr. Gundlach omits this species altogether in his 'Revista,' and still more recently published notes in the 'Journal für Ornithologie' (1875). It may, however, find a place in this paper on the authority of Col. Grayson, who shot it at Mazatlan.

2. CLANGULA ALBEOLA.

Anas albeola, Linn. S. N. i. p. 199 (1766). *Clangula albeola*, Bp. Comp. List, p. 58; Cab. J. für Orn. 1857, p. 230 (Cuba). *Bucephala albeola*, Baird, B. of N. Am. p. 797 ; Gundl. Repert. F.-N. i. p. 390, et J. für Orn. 1875, p. 383 (Cuba).

Hab. Cuba (*Gundlach*).

A specimen of this Duck has been once observed in the market of Havana, and was procured by Gundlach.

* Fleming, it is true, puts *Anas glacialis* first in his list; but *A. clangula* is obviously his type, and therefore we do not use Baird's term *Bucephala*.

Genus 4. ŒDEMIA.

Oedemia, Fleming, Phil. of Zool. ii. p. 260 (1822).
One species only of this northern group is recorded to have been obtained within our limits.

ŒDEMIA PERSPICILLATA.

Anas perspicillata, Linn. S. N. i. p. 201 (1766).
Œdemia perspicillata, Baird, B. of N. Am. p. 806; March, Pr. Ac. Phil. 1864, p. 72 (Jamaica); Scl. et Salv. Nom. Av. Neotrp. p. 130.
Hab. Jamaica (*Gosse*).
The Surf-scoter has been obtained in Jamaica, according to Gosse, only once. March also says it is very rare.

Genus 5. TACHYERES.   Type.

Micropterus, Less. Traité d'Orn. p. 630 (1831) .. *T. cinereus.*
Tachyeres, Owen, Trans. Zool. Soc. ix. p. 254 (1875). *T. cinereus.*

This is a peculiar Antarctic type, rather questionably placed with the other Fuligulinæ *.

TACHYERES CINEREUS.

Anas cinereus, Gm. S. N. p. 506 (1788), ex Pernety (Falklands).
Micropterus cinereus, Gay, Faun. Chil. p. 457 (1848); Gould, P. Z. S. 1859, p. 96 (Falklands); Phil. & Landb. Cat. Av. Chil. p. 43; Scl. P. Z. S. 1860, p. 389 (Falklands); Scl. & Salv. Ibis, 1868, p. 189 (Sandy Point), 1870, p. 499 (Gallegos river), et Nom. Av. Neotr. p. 130; Cunningham, Ibis, 1868, p. 127.
Fuligula cinerea, Schl. Mus. des P.-B., Anseres, p. 13.
Anas brachyptera, Lath. Ind. Orn. ii. p. 834; Q. & G. Voy. Uran. p. 139, t. 39.
Micropterus brachypterus, Eyton, Mon. Anat. p. 144 (1838); Darwin, Voy. Beagle, iii. p. 136 (1841).
Oidemia patachonica, King, P. Z. S. 1830-31, p. 15.
Micropterus patachonicus, Eyton, Mon. Anat. p. 143 (1838); Scl. P. Z. S. 1861, p. 46.
Tachyeres brachypterus, Owen, Trans. Zool. Soc. ix. p. 254.

Grisescenti-brunneus; pectore, hypochondriis, scapularibus et dorso antico cinereo maculatis; gutture rufescente; stria post-oculari et fascia alari albis; abdomine toto clare albo; alis et cauda pure griseis, hujus rectricibus duabus mediis elongatis retrorsum curvatis: long. tota 27·0, alæ 10·8, caudæ 4·5, tarsi 2·4, dig. med. 4·0, rostr. 2·7.

Hab. Falklands (*Pernety, Abbott*); Magellan Straits (*Cunningham*); Chili, Valdivia (*Ph. et Landb.*).
This peculiar Sea-duck, originally discovered in the Falkland Islands, is found also on the west coast of S. America, according to Philippi and Landbeck, from the Straits of Magellan as far north as Valdivia in Chili.

* Cf. Eyton, Mon. Anat. p. 51.

Mr. Darwin, in describing its habits, says that its wings are too
small and weak to allow of flight, but that by their aid, partly swim-
ming and partly flapping the surface of the water, it is enabled to
move very quickly. He adds that he is nearly sure that it moves
its wings alternately instead of, as in the case of other birds, both
together. It is able to dive only a short distance. It feeds on mol-
lusks, obtained from floating kelp and tidal rocks.

Dr. Cunningham remarks that the Loggerhead Duck is very
plentiful in the eastern part of the Straits of Magellan, and that it
also occurs in abundance at the Falkland Islands. He adds that the
bird is exceedingly hard to kill.

In the latter islands Capt. Abbott found them in great numbers,
where they breed along the coast. The nests are readily found by
searching the shore just opposite where the male bird is seen swim-
ming by himself. The old female flutters off to the water, being
quite unable to fly. It lays from the end of September to the end
of November, making its nest in the long grass or a bush of some
kind. The usual complement of eggs is seven, as many as nine
being sometimes found.

The " Flying Loggerhead " is probably the young bird of this
species, though it would appear from Capt. Abbott's remarks that it
breeds when still able to fly; for one flew out of a nest that he
found, high up into the air. Capt. Abbott considers the flying bird
distinct; but Dr. Cunningham's view seems to be the correct one,
viz. that "the so-called *M. patachonicus* is only the young of *M.
cinereus*, the peculiarity being that the power of flight departs from
the bird as it grows old" [*].

The anatomy of this Duck is fully described in Dr. Cunningham's
memoir in the Society's ' Transactions.'

Subfamily V. ERISMATURINÆ.

Genus ERISMATURA.

		Type.
Oxyura, Bp. Syn. N. A. Birds, p. 390 (1828)	......	*E. rubida.*
Gymnura, Nuttall, Man. Ornith. ii. p. 426 (1834)	..	*E. rubida.*
Undina, Gould, B. of Eur. vol. v. pl. 383 (1836)	..	*E. mersa.*
Erismatura, Bp. Comp. List, p. 59 (1838)	....	*E. mersa.*
Cerconectes, Wagler, Ibis, 1832, p. 282	....	*E. mersa.*
Bythonessa, Gloger, Handb. d. Nat. p. 472 (1842)	..	*E. mersa.*

Of the three species of this quasi-cosmopolitan group one is only
found in the northern part of the Neotropical region, a second is very
widely spread in tropical America, and the third may be regarded as
an Antarctic form.

1. ERISMATURA RUBIDA.

Anas rubida, Wils. Am. Orn. vii. p. 128, t. 81 (1814).
Erismatura rubida, Bp. Comp. List, p. 59; Baird, Bird of N. A.
p. 811; Eyton. Mon. Anat. p. 171; Gundl. Repert. F.-N. i. p. 390,
et J. für Orn. 1875, p. 384 (Cuba); Cab. J. für Orn. 1857, p. 230

* See P. Z. S. 1871, p. 262, and Trans. Zool. Soc. vii. 493.

(Cuba); Scl. & Salv. Ibis, 1859, p. 231 (Guatemala) et Nom. Av.
Neotr. p. 136; Scl. P. Z. S. 1859, p. 393 (Mexico); Lawr. Mem.
Boston Soc. N. II. ii. p. 315 (Mexico).
Biziura rubida, Schl. Mus. des P.-B., Anseres, p. 11.
Jamaica Shoveler, Lath. Syn. iii. pt. 2, p. 513, undè
Anas jamaicensis, Gm. S. N. i. p. 529; Lath. Ind. p. 857, et
Vieill. Enc. Méth. p. 127 (1823) (?).

Hab. Cuba (*Gundlach*); Mexico, Oaxaca (*Boucard*); Tepic
(*Grayson*); Guatemela, Lake of Dueñas (*Salvin*).

Although certainly resident in Cuba, this is a rare species. Dr.
Gundlach has found it only in the neighbourhood of Havana.
Salvin met with it breeding on the Lake of Dueñas in Guatemala,
where it is the only Duck resident throughout the year. He observed that it diminished in numbers during the period of the spring
migration. It builds in May amongst the reeds on the margin of
the lake, making a nest of dead flag with a little down. The eggs
are rough in texture, and much resemble those of the European
E. mersa.

2. ERISMATURA FERRUGINEA.

Erismatura ferruginea, Eyton, Mon. Anat. p. 170 (1838)(Chili);
Gray, List Gallinæ &c. (1844), p. 146; Gray & Mitch. Gen. B.
t. 169 (1844) : Bridges, P. Z. S. 1843, p. 119 (Lake of Quintero,
Chili); Gay, Faun. Chil. p. 458 (1848); Bibra, Denksch. Ak.
Wien. v. p. 131, et J. für Orn. 1855, p. 57; Cassin, Gilliss's Exp.
ii. p. 204; Phil. & Landb. Cat. Av. Chil. p. 43, et 1872, p. 549
(Rio Negro); Scl. P. Z. S. 1867, p. 335 (Chili); Scl. & Salv. P. Z. S.
1868, p. 177 (S. Peru), et Nom. Av. Neotr. p. 131; Burm. P. Z. S.
1872, p. 369; Taczanowski, P. Z. S. 1874, p. 554.
Biziura ferruginea, Schl. Mus. des P.-B., Anseres, p. 10.
Erismatura vittata, Ph. & Landb. Wiegm. Arch. 1860, p. 26
(Chili); Scl. P. Z. S. 1867, p. 335.
Erismatura cyanorhyncha, Licht. M.S. (teste Burmeister).

*Supra castanea, capite et collo toto nigris; alis et cauda fuscis;
subtus sordide alba, fusco irrorata, pectore et hypochondriis
castaneis corpore concoloribus; rostro cæruleo, pedibus fuscis:
long. tota 16·0, alæ 5·5, caudæ 3·8, tarsi 1·2, rostri a rictu 1·6.
Fem. fusca, cervino (præcipue in dorso et pileo) irregulariter
transfasciata; vitta suboculari albida; subtus sordide alba,
fusco (præcipue in pectore et in hypochondriis) transvittata.*

Hab. Central Peru (*Nation, Jelski*); S. Peru (*Whitely*); Chili
(*Bridges, Phil. et Landb.*); Buenos Ayres (*Burm.*); Rio Negro
(*Hudson*).

This *Erismatura* was first obtained in Chili by Mr. C. Crawley,
and described by Eyton from his specimens in the British Museum.
Philippi and Landbeck state it is common on all the lakes of the
Central Provinces. They at one time described the female as of a different species (*E. vittata*), but subsequently acknowledged their error
(see P. Z. S. 1868, p. 531). From Chili this species spreads north-

wards along the Andes as far as Central Peru, where Jelski observed
it breeding on the Lake of Junin, and obtained skins and eggs. It
likewise crosses the Andes into the Argentine Republic, as Burmeister met with it on the Laguna Matanza, near Buenos Ayres, and
Mr. Hudson collected examples on the Rio Negro.

3. ERISMATURA DOMINICA.

Anasquerquedula dominicensis, Briss. Orn. vi. p. 472 (S. Domingo),
undè
  Anas dominica, Linn. S. N. i. p. 201 (1766); Max. Beitr. iv.
p. 938 (Bahia); Burm. Syst. Ueb. iii. p. 439 (Lakes of S.E.
Brazil).
  Erismatura dominica, Eyton, Mon. Anat. p. 172 (1838); Cab.
J. für Orn. 1857, p. 231 (Cuba); Gundl. Repert. F.-N. i. p. 391,
et J. für Orn. 1875, p. 384 (Cuba); A. & E. Newton, Ibis, 1859,
p. 367 (St. Croix?); Scl. P.Z.S. 1857, p. 206 (Jalapa), et 1860,
p. 251 (Orizaba); Léot. Ois. Trin. p. 525 (1866) (Trinidad); Pelz.
Orn. Bras. p. 320 (1870); Reinh. Fugl. Bras. Camp. p. 20 (1870)
(Lagoa dos Pitos); Lee, Ibis, 1873, p. 137 (Entrerios); Lawr. Mem.
Boston Soc. N. II. ii. p. 316 (Mexico).
  Biziura dominica, Schl. Mus. des P.-B. Anseres, p. 9.
  Sarcelle de la Guadeloupe, Buff. Pl. Enl. 967 (♀), undè
  Anas spinosa, Gm. S. N. i. p. 522 (1788) (Cayenne et Guiana);
D'Orb. in La Sagra's Cuba, Aves, p. 201 (Cuba et Bolivia).
  Erismatura spinosa, Gosse, Birds Jam. p. 404 (Jamaica).
  "*Erismatura ortygoides*, Hill," Gosse, Birds Jam. p. 406, et Ill.
pl. 113.

> *Ferruginea, nigro variegata et maculata; pileo nigro, vitta super-*
> *ciliari et altera suboculari, cum mento et genis infimis, albidis*
> *nigro punctatis; alis fuscis plaga magna secundariorum alba;*
> *cauda nigra; abdomine sordide albo rufescente irrorato; axil-*
> *laribus pure albis; rostro cæruleo, pedibus nigris: long. tota*
> *13·0, alæ 5·5, caudæ 3·8, tarsi 1 0, rostri a rictu 1·5. Fem.*
> *fusco-nigra, dorso cervino maculato; capitis lateribus et cor-*
> *pore subtus cervinis, illo nigro bivittato; pectore nigro varie-*
> *gato.*

Hab. Cuba (*Gundlach*); S. Domingo (*Briss.*); Jamaica (*Gosse*);
S. Croix (*Newton*); Trinidad (*Léotaud*); Mexico, Jalapa (*Sallé*);
Tepic (*Grayson*); Veragua (*Arcé*); S.E. Brazil (*Max. et Burm.*);
Mattodentro et São Paulo (*Natt.*); Uruguay (*Sellow*); Entrerios
(*Lee*); Bolivia, Chiquitos (*D'Orb.*)
  Obs. Ab *E. rubida* et *E. ferruginea* crassitie minore, dorso variegato et macula alari alba prorsus distinguenda.
  This species of *Erismatura* is widely diffused in Tropical America,
from Mexico and the Antilles down to Uruguay, inhabiting the freshwater lakes like other members of the genus. It nests in Cuba,
where Dr. Gundlach says it is common, resident, and an excellent
diver. Mr. Gosse noticed this species in a broad piece of water
near Redonda, in Jamaica, where as many as three may be seen at one
time. They appear to be tame, but when alarmed sink rather than

dive into the water. They seldom fly, and then only with a heavy laboured flight. The bird referred to by Mr. Gosse as the Quail-duck, or *E. ortygoides* of Mr. Hill, is the male of this species.

Mr. A. Newton describes what he believes to have been a flock of this Duck in St. Croix. He observed them for some time, but was unable to obtain a specimen. Léotaud tells us it is not rare in Trinidad.

In Central America this Lake-duck occurs as far north as the neighbourhood of Mazatlan, where Col. Grayson obtained it, and Jalapa, where Sallé collected specimens. Further south, down the Isthmus, it has not yet been recorded; but Salvin has recently received a skin obtained by Arcé somewhere in Veragua.

We have no recent testimony as to the occurrence of this species in Guiana and Amazonia; but in South and Central Brazil it appears to be found in all the freshwater lakes. In Entrerios it was obtained by Mr. Lee near Gualeguaychu, and in the adjoining republic of Uruguay by Sellow. In La Sagra's 'Cuba' D'Orbigny mentions that he procured examples of it in the small lakes of the province of Chiquitos in Bolivia, its furthest known range in this direction.

Subfamily VI. MERGANETTINÆ.

The Torrent-ducks form a peculiar and somewhat isolated group of the Anatidæ, restricted to the Andes of South America from Colombia to Chili.

<table>
<tr><td>Genus MERGANETTA.</td><td>Type.</td></tr>
</table>

Merganetta, Gould, P. Z. S. 1841, p. 95 .... *M. chilensis.*
Raphipterus, Gay, Faun. Chil. p. 459 (1848) .... *M. chilensis.*

The three species may be diagnosed from the male dress as follows :—

a. Gutture nigro .... 1. *armata.*
b. Gutture albo.
    Ventre nigro, medialiter fusco variegato .... 2. *turneri.*
    Ventre albo griseo flammulato .... 3. *leucogenys.*

In the females the under surface is of a uniform chestnut-red.

1. MERGANETTA ARMATA.

Merganetta armata, Gould, P. Z. S. 1841, p. 95 (Chile); Des Murs, Icon. Orn. t. 48 ♀ (Chili); Gray & Mitch. Gen. of B. t. 170 (♂); Bibra, Denkschr. Akad. Wien, v. p. 132, et J. für Orn. 1855, p. 37; Cassin in Gilliss's Exp. ii. p. 204 (1856); Scl. P. Z. S. 1867, p. 310; Scl. & Salv. Ex. Orn. p. 200, et Nom. Av. Neotr. p. 131

Biziura armata, Schl. Mus. des P.-B., Anseres, p. 12.

Raphipterus chilensis, Gay, Faun. Chil. p. 459 (1848); Phil. & Landb. Cat. Av. Chil. p. 43.

Merganetta chilensis, Des Murs, Icon. Orn. t. 5 (♂).

Supra nigra, plumis albo utrinque marginatis; capite colloque postico et laterali albis, pileo medio in strigam nuchalem pro-

*ducto et linea utrinque ab oculis ad collum imum descendente
nigris ; alis extus cœrulescenti-schistaceis ; tectricibus et secundariis albo anguste terminatis, speculo alari æneo-viridi ; dorso
postico cinereo, uropygio fasciolis minutis albis variegato ;
subtus rufescenti-ochracea, lineis nigris ornata ; mento, linea
ad rostri basin, spatio suboculari cum gutture conjuncto et pectore superiore utraque ex parte nigerrimis ; rostro flavo, pedibus
rubellis : long. tota 16·5, alæ 7, caudæ 4·5, rostri a rictu 1·6,
tarsi 1·9.   Fem. supra ardesiaca, dorsi plumis nigro flammulatis ; collo et uropygio lineis albis nigrisque vermiculatis ;
subtus omnino castanea.*

Hab. Rivers of the Chilian Andes (*Bridges, Gay*).

We are indebted to the researches of Mr. Bridges among the Chilian Andes for the discovery of this curious form.   He sent home
specimens of the present species in 1841, which were described by
Mr. Gould before this Society in November of that year. Mr. Bridges
remarks that it swims and dives against the flow of the Chilian
mountain-torrents with a rapidity truly astonishing.

2. MERGANETTA TURNERI.

Merganetta turneri, Scl. & Salv. P. Z. S. 1869, p. 600 (Peru),
Ex. Orn. p. 199, t. 100, et Nomencl. p. 131.

Merganetta leucogenys, Scl. & Salv. (nec Tsch.) P. Z. S. 1869,
p. 157.

*Supra nigra, interscapulio et scapularibus rufo marginatis ; capite
colloque toto albis, linea rostrum cingente, pileo medio in strigam
nuchalem producto et linea utrinque ad imum collum descendente
nigerrimis ; alis extus cœrulescenti-cinereis ; speculo alari æneo-
viridi ; tectricibus alarum et secundariis albo anguste terminatis ; abdomine nigro, ventre medio fusco variegato ; crisso et
uropygio nigris, albo minute vermiculatis ; cauda fuscescenti-
cinerea unicolori ; tectricibus subalaribus cinereis ; rostro et
pedibus obscure rubris : long. tota 16·0, alæ 7·5, caudæ 5·0,
rostri a rictu 1·5, tarsi 1·8, digiti medii cum ungue 2·3.
Fem. supra cinerea, lateribus cervicis et uropygio albo nigroque
minute vermiculatis ; dorso nigro flammulato ; alis albo bifas-
ciatis ; speculo alari obscure æneo-viridi ; subtus fulvo rufa
unicolor : long. tota 16·0, alæ 6·4, caudæ 4·0, rostri a rictu 1·35.*

Hab. S. Peru ; Rivers of the Cuzcan Andes (*Whitely*).

When we first received examples of this bird from Mr. H. Whitely
we referred it to the species described by Tschudi as *Merganetta
leucogenys.*   Having, however, made a reinvestigation of the group,
we convinced ourselves that Tschudi's bird is, so far as can be de-
cided by his figure and description, inseparable from the *Merganetta
columbiana* of New Granada, and that the present species must be
regarded as undescribed, being equally distinct from the New-Granadan form, and from the Chilian *Merganetta armata.*   From the
former it differs in its larger size, and black breast and flanks, which
are only relieved by some brownish marks in the middle of the belly.
In the New-Granadan bird, which is well represented in Des Murs's

'Iconographie' (tab. vi.), the whole abdomen is white, sparingly striped with narrow blackish markings, and the bill is narrower and much less elevated than in this species. *Merganetta armata*, of which an excellent figure will be found in Gray and Mitchell's 'Genera of Birds,' resembles the present bird in having a black breast; but the edges of the scapularies are white instead of rufous, and the throat and fore neck are black, instead of being pure white as in its two northern allies. It would seem, therefore, that this species occupies an intermediate position as regards the differential characters of the male, just as it does in geographical range, between the two known species. As regards the female, our specimen does not appear to differ in colour from the corresponding sex of *Merganetta armata* (Des Murs, Icon. t. xlviii.).

3. MERGANETTA LEUCOGENYS.

Anas leucogenys, Tsch. Wiegm. Arch. 1843, p. 390.
Erismatura leucogenys, Tsch. Faun. Peru. p. 311, t. xxxvi.
Merganetta leucogenys, Scl. & Salv. Ex. Orn. p. 200; P. Z. S. 1869, p. 601, et 1874, p. 679, et Nomencl. p. 131; Tacz. P. Z. S. 1874, p. 554.
Merganetta columbiana, Des Murs, Rev. Zool. 1845, p. 179, et Icon. Orn. t. 6; Scl. P. Z. S. 1855, p. 161 (Bogotá).

Supra cinerea, dorsi plumis nigris rufescente utrinque marginatis; uropygio fasciolis minutis albis nigrisque variegato; capite colloque toto albis, linea circum rostrum, pileo medio in strigam nuchalem producto et linea ab oculis ad collum imum utrinque descendente nigerrimis; alis cærulescenti-schistaceis, tectricibus et secundariis albo anguste marginatis; speculo alari æneo-viridi; abdomine albo obsolete nigro striolato; rostri flavi culmine nigricante, pedibus rubellis: long. tota 12·5, *alæ* 6·0, *caudæ* 4·5, *rostri a rictu* 1·4, *tarsi* 1·5. Fem. *supra cinerea, dorso nigro flammulato; genis, cervicis lateribus et corpore toto inferiore fulvo-rufis unicoloribus: long. tota* 15·5, *alæ* 5·3, *caudæ* 4, *tarsi* 1·5, *rostri a rictu* 1·4.*

Hab. Columbian Andes near Bogotá (*Goudot*); Quindiu range (*Salmon*); Ecuador (*Mus. S.-G.*); Central Peru (*Tschudi et Jelski*).

This *Merganetta* was originally discovered by Goudot, a well-known French collector, in the neighbourhood of Bogotá. There is a skin in Salvin and Godman's collection from Ecuador; and Tschudi and Jelski obtained it in Central Peru.

Subfamily VII. MERGINÆ.

Genus MERGUS.   Type.

Mergus, Linn. S. N. i. p. 207 (1766) . . . . *M. cucullatus.*
Lophodytes, Reich. Av. Syst. Nat. p. ix. (1852) *M. cucullatus.*

Besides the Hooded Merganser, which occasionally intrudes from the north, one peculiar endemic species of this group is found in the Neotropical region.

1. MERGUS CUCULLATUS.

Mergus cucullatus, Linn. S. N. i. p. 207 (1766); Cab. J. für
Orn. 1857, p. 231 (Cuba); Scl. et Salv. Nom. Av. Neotr. p. 131.
Lophodytes cucullatus, Baird, B. of N. Am. p. 816; Gundl. Repert.
F.-N. i. p. 391, et J. für Orn. 1875, p. 385 (Cuba); Sclater, P. Z. S.
1859, p. 369 (Jalapa).

Hab. Cuba (Gundlach); Mexico (*De Oca*).

The Hooded Merganser is of rare occurrence on passage in Cuba,
and does not appear to have been noted elsewhere within our limits,
except in South-eastern Mexico.

2. MERGUS OCTOSETACEUS.

Mergus octosetaceus, Vieill. N. D. xiv. p. 222 (1817), et Enc.
Méth. p. 351 (1823) (Brazil).
Mergus brasilianus, Vieill. Gal. des Ois. ii. p. 209, t. 283 (1834);
Eyton, Mon. Anat. p. 176 (1838); Burm. Syst. Ueb. iii. p. 441;
Pelz. Orn. Bras. p. 322 (1870); Schl. Mus. des P.-B. *Anseres,* p. 6;
Scl. et Salv. Nom. Av. Neotr. p. 131.
Mergus fuscus, Licht. Doubl. p. 85 (1823).
Mergus lophotes, Cuv. MS. (teste Schlegel).

Supra fusco-niger purpureo vix tinctus; plaga alarum duplici,
fascia nigra divisa, alba; cervice postica æneo micante; pileo
et crista elongata tenui saturate fumoso-nigris; abdomine satu-
rate cinereo, fasciis numerosis albis in ventre signato; cervice
antica et pectoris lateribus griseo et nigro confertim vermicu-
latis; rostro nigro, pedibus flavidis; long. tota 19·0, *alæ* 7·2,
caudæ 4·0, *tarsi* 1·4, *rostri a rictu* 2·2.

Hab. S.E. Brazil, São Paulo (*Licht.*); Rio Ytararc (*Natt.*).

This scarce Merganser was first described by Vieillot from Dela-
lande's specimens in the Paris Museum, and subsequently figured by
the same author under another name. Lichtenstein gives São Paulo
as its locality; and Natterer obtained five examples on the River
Ytararc in the southern part of that province in August 1820. One
of these skins, marked as the female sex, is now in the collection of
Salvin and Godman, whence our description is taken.

IV. *Table of the Geographical Distribution of the Neotropical Anatidæ, with remarks thereon.*

On referring to the last column of the Table (pp. 410 & 411), it
will be seen that out of the 62 species of Anatidæ included in the
Neotropical list 25 are likewise found in North America. Of these
25, however, two (*Dendrocygna fulva* and *Querquedula cyanoptera*)
are visitors from the south; and the Nearctic species which intrude
into the Neotropical region (mostly in winter) are, so far as is at
present known, 23 in number, namely

Anser hyperboreus,	Anas boschas,
—— cærulescens,	—— obscura,
—— gambeli,	—— strepera,
Bernicla canadensis,	Querquedula carolinensis.

Querquedula discors,
Dafila acuta,
Mareca americana,
Spatula clypeata,
Aix sponsa,
Fuligula marila,
—— *affinis,*
—— *collaris,*

Fuligula americana,
—— *valisneria,*
Clangula glaucion,
—— *albeola,*
Œdemia perspicillata,
Erismatura rubida,
Mergus cucullatus.

Deducting these 23, there remain 39 in the purely Neotropical list, which may be divided as follows.

In the first place, the genera *Chenalopex*, *Dendrocygna*, *Sarcidiornis*, and *Cairina* are essentially tropicopolitan. We may therefore associate the birds of these genera together as an intertropical division containing eight species, namely

Chenalopex jubata,
Dendrocygna fulva,
—— *autumnalis,*
—— *discolor,*

Dendrocygna arborea,
—— *viduata,*
Sarcidiornis melanonota,
Cairina moschata.

	Falkland Islands.	Tierra del Fuego and Patagonia.	Chili.	Argent. Republ.	Paraguay.	S. Brazil.	Bolivia.	Peru.	Amazonia.	Guiana.	Venezuela and Trinidad.	U. S. of Colombia.	Ecuador.	Galapagos Islands.	Central America and Mexico.	Antilles.	N. America.
1. Anser hyperboreus																*	*
2. —— cærulescens																*	*
3. —— gambeli															*	*	*
4. Bernicla canadensis															*	*	*
*5. —— melanoptera			*				*	*									
*6. —— magellanica	*	*															
*7. —— dispar	*	*															
*8. —— poliocephala	*	*	*														
*9. —— rubidiceps		*															
*10. —— antarctica	*	*															
*11. Chenalopex jubata									*		*						
*12. Cygnus nigricollis	*	*	*	*		*											
*13. —— coscoroba	*	*	*	*													
*14. Dendrocygna fulva						*	*		*						*		*
*15. —— autumnalis									*						*		
*16. —— discolor									*		*				*		
*17. —— arborea																*	
*18. —— viduata						*			*	*	*					*	
*19. Sarcidiornis carunculata						*			*	*	*						
*20. Cairina moschata						*			*		*				*		
21. Anas boschas															*	*	*
22. —— obscura																*	*
*23. —— specularis	*	*															
*24. —— cristata	*	*	*				*	*									
	7	8	7	3	4	5	2	2	4	3	5	1	0	0	7	8	7

	Falkland Islands.	Tierra del Fuego and Patagonia.	Chili.	Argent. Republic.	Paraguay.	S. Brazil.	Bolivia.	Peru.	Amazonia.	Guiana.	Venezuela and Trinidad.	U.S. of Colombia.	Ecuador.	Galapagos Islands.	Central America and Mexico.	Antilles.	N. America.
	7	8	7	3	4	5	2	2	4	3	5	1	0	0	7	8	7
25. Anas strepera															*	*	*
*26. Heteronetta melanocephala			*	*													
27. Querquedula discors											*				*	*	*
*28. —— cyanoptera	*	*	*	*								*			*		*
29. —— carolinensis															*	*	*
*30. —— oxyptera								*									
*31. —— flavirostris	*	*	*	*													
*32. —— andium												*					
*33. —— versicolor	*	*	*									*					
*34. —— puna							*	*									
*35. —— torquata			*														
*36. —— brasiliensis	*		*	*	*	*											
37. Dafila acuta															*	*	*
*38. —— spinicauda	*	*	*	*													
*39. —— bahamensis	*		*	*		*			*		*						
40. Mareca americana											*				*	*	*
*41. —— sibilatrix	*	*	*	*													
42. Spatula clypeata											*				*	*	*
*43. —— platalea	*		*	*													
44. Aix sponsa															*	*	*
*45. Metopiana peposaca			*	*													
46. Fuligula marila											*				*		*
47. —— affinis											*				*	*	*
48. —— collaris															*	*	*
49. —— americana															*	*	*
50. —— valisneria															*	*	*
51. Clangula glaucion															*	*	*
52. —— albeola															*	*	*
53. Œdemia perspicillata																*	*
*54. Tachyeres cinereus	*	*															
55. Erismatura rubida															*	*	*
*56. —— ferruginea			*	*	*												
*57. —— dominica						*	*		*	*	*				*		
*58. Merganetta armata			*														
*59. —— turneri								*									
*60. —— leucogenys								*			*	*					
61. Mergus cucullatus															*	*	*
*62. —— octosetaceus						*											
	15	15	18	14	5	9	5	7	5	5	10	3	2	2	25	25	25

Secondly, the quasi-cosmopolitan genus *Erismatura* has 2 representatives peculiar to the Neotropical region—namely, *E. ferruginea* and *E. dominicana*.

After deducting these two categories, the remaining 29 species form the Antarctic division of the Neotropical Anatidæ, and consist mostly of species belonging to genera also found in the north—e. g. *Bernicla* (6), *Cygnus* (2), *Anas* (2), *Querquedula* (8), *Dafila* (2), *Mareca* (1), *Spatula* (1), and *Mergus* (1). Adding these together,

we have the following 23 species of Neotropical Anatidæ belonging
to genera also met with in the north—namely

Bernicla melanoptera,
—— *magellanica,*
—— *dispar,*
—— *poliocephala,*
—— *rubidiceps,*
—— *antarctica,*
Cygnus nigricollis,
—— *coscoroba,*
Anas specularis,
—— *cristata,*
Querquedula cyanoptera,
—— *oxyptera,*

Querquedula flavirostris,
—— *andium,*
—— *versicolor,*
—— *puna,*
—— *torquata,*
—— *brasiliensis,*
Dafila spinicauda,
—— *bahamensis,*
Mareca sibilotrix,
Spatula platalea,
Mergus octosetaceus.

Lastly, there are 4 generic forms of Anatidæ peculiar to the
Antarctic portion of the Neotropical region (*Heteronetta, Metopiana, Tachyeres,* and *Merganetta*), embracing the following six
species—

Heteronetta melanocephala,
Metopiana peposaca,
Tachyeres cinereus,

Merganetta armata,
—— *turneri,*
—— *leucogenys.*

The Neotropical Anatidæ may therefore be summarized as
follows :—

A. Nearctic species, mostly occurring only in
    winter within the Neotropical Region   23
B. Neotropical species.
    a. Species belonging to Tropicopolitan
        genera   8
    b. Representatives of a Cosmopolitan
        genus   2
    c. Peculiar species of genera also Arctic..   23
    d. Species of peculiar Antarctic genera..   6
                            ——39

                            —
                          62

www.ingramcontent.com/pod-product-compliance
Lightning Source LLC
Chambersburg PA
CBHW021635270326
41931CB00008B/1035